Railway Memories

HALIFAX
&
THE CALDER VALLEY

Jack Wild & Stephen Chapman

BELLCODE BOOKS
10 RIDGE BANK
TODMORDEN
WEST YORKSHIRE OL14 7BA

One of Calderdale's great climbs. Jubilee 4-6-0 No. 45739 *Ulster* crosses Stansfield Hall Junction, Todmorden, at the foot of the four-mile slog up to Copy Pit, with the 9.35am Bradford-Blackpool special on Easter Monday, 1966. The engine was in terrible condition, typical of many near the end of steam, and reached Copy Pit summit at walking pace. *(Robert Anderson)*

Copyright © 1998 Bellcode Books
ISBN 1 871233 10 0
All rights reserved. The contents of this book are the copyright of Bellcode Books and their contributors and may not be reproduced in any form without the prior written consent of the copyright holder.
Edited by Stephen Chapman
Printed by The Amadeus Press Ltd., Huddersfield.

FRONTICEPIECE: Stanier Black Five 4-6-0 No. 44746, one of those fitted with Caprotti valve gear, makes a powerful image as it attacks the last few yards to Summit Tunnel with the 11.15am Scarborough to Liverpool Exchange express on 25th August, 1962. *(Robert Anderson)*

FRONT COVER: The famous Wainhouse Tower looks down from a Halifax hilltop as immaculately turned out Jubilee 4-6-0 No. 45694 *Bellerophon* calls at Sowerby Bridge - once the main railway operating centre of Calderdale - with a westbound special in June, 1965 *(Jack Wild)*

BACK COVER TOP: Beacon Hill towers above as Fairburn Class 4 2-6-4T No. 42107 of Low Moor depot leaves Halifax station with a Bradford-Stockport express on 21st October, 1963. *(Jack Wild)*

BACK COVER BOTTOM: One of Calderdale's memorable workings was the Newcastle-Manchester train of empty newspaper vans. This was its last run on 25th June, 1988, crossing Gauxholme Viaduct hauled by Great Western liveried Class 47 No. 47628 *Sir Daniel Gooch.* *(Stephen Chapman)*

In steam days not only were the Newcastle to Manchester Red Bank empty news vans usually double-headed but they produced fascinating combinations of locomotives. In this case Warrington Dallam Jubilee 4-6-0 No. 45590 *Travancore* and a Black Five power the train past the Co-op flour mills at Sowerby Bridge in February, 1965. (*Jack Wild / Stephen Chapman collection*)

INTRODUCTION

As summer 1968 approached, a grubby, worn-out steam engine at Todmorden became a magnet for railway enthusiasts all over Britain.

The Copy Pit banker, a 25 year old Stanier 8F 2-8-0 from Rose Grove engine sheds in Burnley, was one of the very last regular steam locomotive duties on the whole of British Rail.

Its job was to push heavy freight trains bound for Lancashire up the four-mile slog to Copy Pit summit and, if the train's own engine was also one of the last steam survivors, it made one of the last great steam spectaculars in Britain.

Before the summer was out, it had all ended and so too had a whole era. Over the following years, the traditions of a century were swept away forever by rationalisation, resignalling and a massive, sickening loss of freight traffic.

Railway Memories No. 11 takes us back to a glorious time when Calderdale's railways carried top link expresses, Saturday excursions packed with holidaymakers bound for Blackpool, and a seemingly endless procession of freight; when branch lines sprouted in all directions, when Heckmondwike, Cleckheaton, Brighouse and Ripponden all had a place on the rail network, when trains left Halifax for Bradford and Keighley "over the Alps", and the days when Sowerby Bridge, Mytholmroyd and

Contents

Mirfield were important railway centres.

Because there have been so many changes since those that immediately followed 1968 - some good, some bad, some earth-shattering - we include a section devoted to more recent events which are now also railway memories.

Railway Memories No. 11 extends east to Healey Mills where it joins Railway Memories No. 6, and north to Low Moor and Queensbury where it meets Railway Memories Nos.4 and 7, providing continuous coverage of the one-time rail system across much of West Yorkshire.

SETTING THE SCENE

Nestling in deep valleys shaded by wooded slopes is an industrial region where the chimneys of countless textile mills do their best to outreach the wild and rugged hills that rise up around them. Railways wind their way tortuously up hill and down dale, negotiating a succession of high viaducts and deep tunnels in their effort to serve communities that derive their livlihoods from spinning, weaving, mining, engineering and farming. An important trunk line threads the main east-west valley connecting two great industrial regions with expresses and heavy goods trains.

This was Calderdale, West Yorkshire, unique in character and unique in terms of its railways.

Nowadays, its rail system is much reduced and the mill chimneys are almost gone, but not so long ago it was a hive of railway activity.

The Main Line

The most important railway through Calderdale has always been the historic route of the Manchester and Leeds Railway - the Calder Valley Main Line.

Running from Manchester to Normanton where it connected with the North Midland Railway into Leeds, the M&L was the first railway across the Pennines. Its engineer, George Stephenson, designed the line to be as level as possible and its construction involved extensive civil engineering works.

The line took nearly five years to complete, the final section between Hebden Bridge and Littleborough being opened in March, 1841, after the construction of seven tunnels and three viaducts in 10 miles.

These included the infamous Summit Tunnel through the Pennine watershed. Taking three years to build and claiming nine lives in the process, it was, at 1 mile 1125 yards, for a short time the world's longest railway tunnel.

All the other tunnels are fairly short but the first of three substantial viaducts encountered around Todmorden as the train rolls down from Summit Tunnel is the rambling Gauxholme Viaduct, its 18 spans taking the railway over a tributary valley and one of several crossings of the Rochdale Canal. It immediately recrosses the canal on a bowstring girder bridge with four castellated turrets. The nine-arch Todmorden Viaduct carries the line 55ft above the town centre; then comes the five-arch Lob Mill Viaduct, sandwiched between two tunnels.

Apart from the huge challenge which building these structures posed, there were unexpected problems. East of Summit Tunnel the engineers encountered silt so deep that they had to support the railway on 200ft timber piles soaked in pitch. Nearer Hebden Bridge, attempts to tunnel through an outcrop at Charlestown were abandoned because the ground was too unstable so the line was built on a sharp curve around the obstruction. It was rebuilt through a cutting and the curve abandoned after a major accident there in 1912.

The M&L by-passed Halifax, much to the annoyance of the increasingly influential business community there, but in 1844 a branch was completed from an east-facing junction at North Dean(Greetland). In just 1.75 miles it crossed over the River Calder on a viaduct, climbed the Hebble Valley at 1 in 53/45, passed through a 91-yard tunnel and negotiated a sheer rock cutting to reach its Halifax terminus at Shaw Syke.

Three years later, the Manchester and Leeds became the Lancashire and Yorkshire Railway embracing a network eventually linking all the two counties' major towns, cities and ports.

By 1850 the L&Y had completed a line from Todmorden to Rose Grove, Burnley, where it connected with the East Lancashire Railway, creating a through route to Preston.

Another heavily engineered line taking four years to build, it includes three tunnels, the lofty 13-arch Lydgate Viaduct and a curving climb up 2.5 miles at 1 in 65 and another mile at 1 in 80/77 to Copy Pit Summit, 749ft above sea level. From there it descends towards Burnley at 1 in 68-71. An east facing connection laid at Todmorden in 1862 allowed trains to run direct between Yorkshire and Preston.

The M&L main line reaches its highest spot, 540ft above sea level, inside Summit Tunnel after which it descends a steady 1 in 180 to Charlestown, changing direction from south-north to west-east and describing almost a complete semi-circle. On the way are some breathtaking views of the local Pennine scene. Beneath Gauxholme Viaduct is a succession of canal locks and to the east the Gothic spire of Todmorden Unitarian Church. From Todmorden Viaduct passengers can look down on the market place and town hall once bisected by the Yorkshire/Lancashire border, or up the valley towards Burnley, a source of magnificent scenery for Copy Pit line travellers.

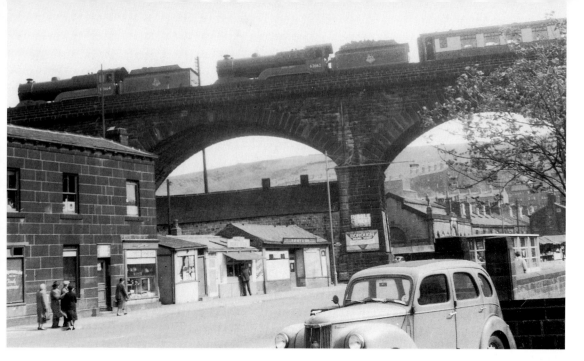

Fifty five feet above Burnley Road in the centre of Todmorden, a pair of real strangers, ex-Great Central D11/1 4-4-0s Nos. 62664 *Princess Mary* and 62662 *Prince of Wales* cross the soot-stained viaduct after stopping for water in the station. The date was 12th May, 1956 and they were working the eastbound Ian Allan Pennine Pullman railtour.

From Lydgate Viaduct they can look back down the valley towards Todmorden or upwards to Eagle Rock - a natural rock formation in the shape of an eagle. Approaching Copy Pit one of the two streams that meet under the centre of Todmorden to form the River Calder tumbles down the hillside to join the railway. Beyond the summit are panoramic views across open country towards the 1,827ft Pendle Hill, haunt of the Lancashire witches.

Around Todmorden, frequent glimpses can be had between the tunnels and trees of Calderdale's most prominent landmark, the stone obelisk that reaches skyward from the 1,300ft Stoodley Pike. Going east, the valley closes in, granting only brief openings where tributaries meet, as at Hebden Bridge and Mytholmroyd. At Sowerby Bridge the town below sits astride the still rushing river, while boatyards mark the meeting of the Rochdale and the Calder and Hebble canals. East of Greetland, the Pennines recede and the valley widens out. The railway continues its easterly course through Brighouse and Mirfield, crossing the recrossing the winding river as it goes.

Until the 1970s, the line held considerable railway interest. Sowerby Bridge, now an unstaffed halt - its substantial platform canopies clinging to a greater past - was Calderdale's principal operating centre. It had a six-platform station

and a locomotive depot supplying engines for freight and local passenger trains. At Mytholmroyd, where there is now only scrubland and another unstaffed halt, were extensive sidings. There were yards at Greetland, Brighouse and Bradley Wood too. At Luddendenfoot were the water troughs where engines refilled their tanks at speed, and the now disappeared station where Branwell Bronte worked briefly as a clerk for the M & L until his fondness for a tipple in work time found him out. Further east, through Mirfield and Thornhill, was one of the most complex stretches of railway anywhere. West of Mirfield, at Heaton Lodge Junction where the London and North Western line from Huddersfield joins the L&Y, Trans-Pennine expresses passed underneath and crossed the Calder on their way straight to Leeds via the so-called 'New Line' - opened by the LNWR in 1900 to avoid badly congested junctions at Mirfield and Leeds. At Mirfield was another-locomotive depot and more sorting sidings. There were also junctions with the L&Y Spen Valley line from Low Moor and the Midland Railway goods branch to Huddersfield.

After Thornhill LNW Junction, where the LNW route to Leeds via Batley parts company, was Thornhill Junction where the branch came in from Heckmondwike, followed by Thornhill station, then the branch to Dewsbury Market Place, the junction with the Midland line to Royston and finally Healey Mills sidings.

The West Riding Union, Halifax and the Great Northern

Halifax got its first rail link with Manchester in 1850 courtesy of the LNWR which built a spur from the M&L at Bradley Wood, east of Brighouse, to connect with its Huddersfield and Manchester line at Bradley Junction.

With this plan before Parliament in 1846, the M&L began to take notice and helped form the West Riding Union Railway to build not only a Manchester-facing line from Halifax and Bradford, but also the Spen Valley line and a more direct Halifax-Huddersfield route.

The WRU also required considerable engineering works. The first section to open, in July, 1848, was the easier 7.75-mile Spen Valley line, from a west-facing junction on the M&L at Mirfield to Low Moor. Even it included a 1 in 99 gradient north of Heckmondwike. The Low Moor-Bradford section was completed in May, 1850, while the 5.25-mile Low Moor-Halifax section, requiring two long tunnels and a substantial viaduct, followed in August. Halifax got its Manchester-facing connection on 1st January, 1852 when the 2.75 miles down from the M&L

Greetland branch at Dryclough Junction to the main line at Milner Royd was completed. Descending at 1 in 118 it crosses one of Calderdale's most striking railway structures, the 66ft high, 23-arch Copley viaduct.

In November, 1846 the WRU passed to the M&L, and then the L&Y which decided not to proceed with the Huddersfield line and the Heckmondwike-Thornhill bit of the Spen Valley. The Great Northern Railway from London King's Cross was extending to many northern towns and cities and Halifax was one of its targets. But it was happy to rely on running powers and agreements with the L&Y, which even worked its London trains. However, in 1874 it set about building its own lines from Bradford and Keighley by the most difficult route imaginable. The 2.25 miles from Holmfield to Queensbury required a 1033ft long, 60ft deep cutting, the 1 mile 741 yard Queensbury Tunnel, and a 1 in 80 gradient taking the line to over 800ft above sea level. The Queensbury lines took over five years to build and were known to railwaymen as "The Alpine Route."

The final link was the 2.5-mile Halifax and Ovenden Joint Railway from Halifax to Holmfield, opened between 1874 and December, 1879 by which time it was vested jointly in the GN and L&Y. It required a large viaduct between Halifax and North Bridge

The Low Moor-Mirfield line was the first part of the West Riding Union to open but 118 years later it was in decline. Worn-out Jubilee 4-6-0 No. 45739 *Ulster* leaves Heckmondwike, reopened for the day, with the 7.55am Bradford-Bridlington buffet car special on 18th June, 1966. The train was one of three sponsored by the British Belting and Asbestos Company of Cleckheaton. *(Robert Anderson)*

The spectacular Copley Viaduct is still a feature of the West Riding Union line from Milner Royd to Halifax. Jubilee 4-6-0 No. 45565 *Victoria* leaves the main line down below on the left and climbs up to Halifax with a special train in September, 1966. *(Jack Wild / Stephen Chapman collection)*

stations, tunnels through solid rock, and a 1 in 45 climb for two miles up to Holmfield.

The GN began running Halifax-Bradford passenger trains in 1879 and a Halifax-Keighley service in 1884.

Filling the gaps

Dewsbury once had three passenger stations and one of them was the L&Y's at Market Place, terminus of a 1.25-mile branch opened to all traffic in April, 1867. It crossed the Calder on a 135ft-span plate bow girder bridge, joining the main line by a triangular junction where the L&Y set up a carriage and wagon works.

The Thornhill-Heckmondwike line - and its 12-arch viaduct over the Calder - was finally opened in 1869, allowing trains to run direct between Bradford, Dewsbury and Wakefield.

The 1.5-mile Greetland-Stainland branch was added in 1875 and the Sowerby Bridge-Ripponden line three years later. Following the Ryburn Valley, the Ripponden branch was part of a planned high speed cut-off direct to Littleborough, accompanied by a new station on the junction at Sowerby Bridge. The line was extended to Rishworth in 1881 but that was as far as it went. The new Sowerby Bridge station was built but without platforms on the Rishworth branch.

The Pickle Bridge line, successor to the WRU

Huddersfield route, was also opened in 1881. It ran 3.75 miles from Pickle Bridge Junction, on the Halifax-Bradford line near Wyke, to Anchor Pit Junction, east of Brighouse. The new line missed Brighouse station so another was opened in Clifton Road. Its only other station was at Bailiff Bridge. Construction involved considerable earthworks, 1 in 60/70 gradients and the ill-fated Wyke Viaduct.

With the coming of the WRU to Halifax a temporary through station replaced Shaw Syke. The present station with its Italian-style buildings was opened in 1855, wooden buildings from the temporary one being used for a new station at Copley, opened in 1856 to serve Copley Mills factory village.

Halifax station was expanded during the 1880s with extra platforms for the Queensbury trains bringing the total to six (three islands), hydraulic lifts between them, a new approach on a wide bridge over new sidings, and separate L&Y and GN booking offices on each side of the station entrance. The L&Y refreshment rooms were on platform three and the GN on platform five. By the start of the 20th Century, Halifax station had 92 staff and was handling 294 L&Y and 71 GN trains a day.

In 1890 the enlarged station was rechristened Halifax Old because work had already started on another. This was St Paul's, terminus of the three-mile Halifax High Level line, opened in the same year and vested jointly in the GN and L&Y in 1894. It is said that 80,000 tons of coal a year had to be dragged uphill from the existing stations to power an estimated 130 mills in the developing hilltop area to be served by the High Level.

Leaving the Queensbury line at Holmfield, it climbed gradients of 1 in 35/50, cut through an 810-yard solid rock tunnel, crossed the Hebble Brook and Wheatley Valley on a curving 10-arch 100ft high viaduct and negotiated 15 other bridges to reach St Paul's - over 300ft above Halifax Old station.

The final piece in the jigsaw came when the Midland Railway planned a new line direct from its existing main line at Royston Junction to Bradford from where trains could continue to Scotland without having to reverse in Leeds. The only portions actually built, however, were from Royston to the L&Y main line at Thornhill Midland Junction, opened for goods in 1905, and a short steeply-graded branch to a goods station at Dewsbury Savile Town, opened the next year. The Thornhill-Royston line carried Bradford/Halifax-Sheffield expresses from 1909 to 1946 and remained a handy route for coal between Barnsley pits and Lancashire and excursions to the Lancashire coast until 1968.

In 1922 the L&Y was absorbed by the LNWR ready for the 1923 grouping when it merged with the Midland and other companies to form the London Midland and Scottish Railway. The GNR joined with the North Eastern, the Great Central and others to become the London and North Eastern. The Halifax High Level and Halifax & Ovenden became joint LMS/LNER. Nationalisation in 1948 brought everything under British Railways. By 1997 BR had been split up and privatised, infrastucture and operational control going to Railtrack with most passenger services run by Regional Railways North East and most freight by English, Welsh and Scottish Railway.

Industrial railways in the area included a system said to have totalled 50 miles which connected Low Moor iron works with several collieries in the countryside between there and Cleckheaton. Not far away, a smaller system linked the Brookes flagstone company's quarries, mines, works and exchange sidings at Lightcliffe until 1969. High on the tops at Heptonstall, above Hebden Bridge, a 3ft gauge railway with up to 15 locomotives carried workers and materials for the construction of Walshaw Dean resevoirs until 1912. It crossed Blackdean Valley on a 105ft high trestle bridge.

Passenger Traffic

For generations, the regular Leeds/Bradford-Manchester-Liverpool expresses formed the backbone of the region's principal services but there were other notable expresses too.

In 1910 Halifax boasted through trains or coaches to four London termini, Bristol, Bournemouth and Birmingham - even Belfast, Holland and Belgium. Running via Wakefield were the daily 12.30pm Newcastle-Liverpool, 4.53pm Newcastle-Manchester, and 6.55pm Liverpool-Newcastle dining car expresses. Daily Blackburn-King's Cross through coaches ran each way via Copy Pit, calling at Stansfield Hall to serve Todmorden, and there was the 2.10pm Liverpool-Hull Paragon and Riverside Quay. There were also the 5.55am Fleetwood-Bradford/Leeds and 8.10pm Bradford/8.5pm Leeds-Fleetwood "Belfast Boat Train" services, while the 12.13pm York-Manchester conveyed through coaches from Harwich connecting with sailings from Hook of Holland and Antwerp.

The L&Y ran a network of local services that covered almost every permutation of its lines in the area. Cleckheaton, which now has no trains, then had direct services to Bradford, Leeds, Halifax, Dewsbury, Wakefield, Huddersfield and beyond - even Hull and London. Stainland and Rishworth had good services, frequent shuttles connected Dewsbury Market Place with the main line at Thornhill, and Bradford-Huddersfield passengers had three routes to choose from.

GN services included those between Halifax, Queensbury, Bradford and Keighley, and Holmfield-St. Paul's shuttles but it also ran trains over L & Y metals. These included the 12.18pm Halifax-King's Cross and 5.45pm return, both via Cleckheaton. There were Halifax-Leeds Central locals via Low Moor and, at the eastern end of the main line, a Huddersfield-King's Cross express each way. From 1926 until the 1930s Halifax even had a Pullman train from King's Cross - a portion of the West Riding Pullman detached at Wakefield and hauled via Queensbury.

The Great Central in 1910 ran daily 10am and 6.20pm Marylebone-Bradford and 5pm Bradford-Marylebone expresses as well as through carriages attached to Bradford-Penistone trains. They took the Pickle Bridge line to Huddersfield but the 7.47am Halifax-Marylebone and Bristol through carriages went via Cleckheaton and Mirfield. Like the King's Cross trains, they were worked by L&Y

Memories of the Calder Valley's premier trains in the 1950s, the 10.30am Liverpool Exchange to Newcastle dining car express and its corresponding return working. Un-named Patriot 4-6-0 No. 45517 was one of the regular locomotives employed on this service but on 7th August, 1961 it was racing past Luddendenfoot with the 9.40am Liverpool to Leeds and Bradford. *(Robert Anderson)*

engines and men.

The North Eastern ran two trains from Hull to Halifax via Wakefield and Brighouse and two the other way, one via Cleckheaton, as well as a train via Brighouse to Selby.

There were also four daily Midland Halifax-Sheffield trains each way conveying through carriages to/from St. Pancras, Birmingham and Bristol. The 9.10am Bradford-St. Pancras and 4.55pm return "Yorkshireman" via the Spen Valley ran until 1939. In the same pre-war years there were also through carriages to Euston and a Friday night Halifax-Glasgow via Copy Pit and Preston.

At holiday times the railway helped thousands of West Riding families escape the dark satanic mills by running scores of extra trains to the east and west coast resorts, Blackpool, Southport, Scarborough and Bridlington being favourites. During wakes weeks smaller stations like Todmorden and Lightcliffe boasted originating trains. Stations like Rishworth and St. Paul's still handled holiday trains after their regular passenger services had ceased.

By 1961 the more exotic services had disappeared but the Leeds/Bradford-Liverpool expresses still ran, most combining and detaching Leeds and Bradford portions at Low Moor.

The York-Wakefield-Manchester trains were still there but between 1959 and 1961 the Liverpool-Newcastle express which then left Liverpool Exchange at 10.30am had been truncated to run only as far as York - with no dining car - returning from York at 2.2pm.

Halifax still boasted through services to King's Cross in 1961 and through coaches to/from St. Pancras via Barnsley but the last link with Marylebone - the "South Yorkshireman" through train introduced in 1948 - was withdrawn in winter, 1960.

Calder Valley main line local services still consisted of various permutations in the late 1950s and early '60s. The 7.51am Todmorden-Manchester Victoria and 6.47pm Manchester Victoria-Todmorden were especially interesting. The 7.51 used the locomotive - often a Royal Scot 4-6-0 or a Britannia Pacific - from an overnight Glasgow-Manchester train. It was sent light from Manchester to collect the coaches which stabled overnight at Todmorden after arriving on the 6.47pm. Amazingly, these two trains still run in 1998 but are of little interest, being mundane diesel units.

Other local services in 1961 consisted of Bradford-Huddersfield-Penistone/Stockport trains via Halifax or Cleckheaton and Mirfield, and trains between Bradford, Wakefield, Goole and Normanton via Cleckheaton.

In January, 1962 the Liverpool-Leeds/Bradford steam trains gave way to Liverpool-Bradford-Leeds-Harrogate diesel multiple units specially designed for the route. Built by the Birmingham Railway Carriage and Wagon Company they were aptly known as the "Calder Valley" sets. Each 3-car unit had four Rolls Royce 180hp engines instead of the more usual 150hp engines on other DMUs. Superior suspension gave a higher quality ride and a total of 720hp enabled them to cope superbly with the route's toughest gradients. They also took over some direct York services.

By 1968-69 Calderdale's passenger service amounted to little more than the Leeds City-Manchester/Liverpool Exchange expresses and Manchester-Wakefield-York trains operated mainly by the DMUs. Sowerby Bridge was still an interchange and several DMUs started and terminated there. Bradford-Manchester locals supplemented peak-hour expresses.

Other weekday services of note then were the 04.25 Manchester Victoria-York mail, the 17.47 Fridays Only Manchester Exchange-York, switched to the Calder Valley in June, 1967 when still steam, often a Britannia Pacific, and the 04.38 Halifax-Manchester Victoria mail which by May, 1968 was the very last steam passenger train in West Yorkshire. Halifax still had a daily London service, the 08.48 to King's Cross via Wakefield Kirkgate and the 18.53 King's Cross-Bradford which reached Halifax at 22.53 via Huddersfield. Interesting survivors were the 07.45 Normanton to Halifax DMU and the 08.10 Halifax-Normanton-York.

Quite a few summer Saturday and Bank Holiday extras still ran but they were not at the levels of the early '60s.

Factories, mills and businesses still relied on the railway for their goods and in the mornings and evenings especially were various parcels workings. These included Manchester-Todmorden diesel parcels units and the 18.35 Hebden Bridge-Halifax-Normanton. Two newspaper trains ran to Bradford from Huddersfield where they connected with trunk services from Manchester - the 03.06 from Hudersfield being a DMU and tail van which passed Halifax non-stop, and the 03.18 loco-hauled calling Halifax at 04.05. In steam days the most eagerly await-ed train through Calderdale was the daily col-lection of empty newspaper vans going back to Manchester Red Bank sidings, loading up to 20 vehicles and almost always double-headed by combinations of Class 5, B1 or Jubilee 4-6-0s. The Red Bank vans continued running, hauled by a single diesel locomotive, until the newspa-per traffic switched to road in June, 1988.

Present day service patterns were established on 5th January, 1970 when all the direct Manchester-Wakefield-York trains were with-drawn. Sowerby Bridge became just another halt on a standard hourly Leeds-Halifax-Manchester service, but a new service connect-ed Wakefield with Trans-Pennine trains at Huddersfield. Despite a number of threats it survives in 1998 running all the way between Wakefield and Liverpool.

The basic hourly Calder Valley service remained over the following two decades although origins and destinations of trains varied between Leeds, York, Scarborough and

The 7.51am Todmorden to Manchester Victoria stop-ping train frequently used top link power.
Here, Leeds Holbeck Royal Scot 4-6-0 No. 46130 *The West Yorkshire Regiment* sets off from Todmorden on the 25th September, 1961 (*Peter Wood*)

One of the 3-car Calder Valley DMUs approaches Milner Royd Junction while working a Harrogate-Liverpool Exchange service in 1964. *(Jack Wild / Stephen Chapman collection)*

Hull in the east, and Manchester Victoria, Blackpool, Southport and Liverpool Lime Street in the west. One subtle change was that the Leeds-Manchester Victoria DMUs, still designated Class 1 expresses in 1973 were at some stage downgraded to Class 2 stopping trains. By May, 1991 though, the service had been doubled to half-hourly York-Manchester for most of the day with alternate trains to/from Liverpool. In 1998 they alternate between Manchester Victoria-York or Selby, with more between Leeds, Halifax and Hebden Bridge.

Summer Saturday trains are now just history. The last ones through Calderdale, the Sheffield-Blackpool, the Hebden Bridge-Bridlington, the Castleford/Leeds-Blackpool, and the Bradford-Poole ceased in the mid to late 1980s.

During the 1980s, just as passengers were starting to flock back, many Calder Valley DMUs were reduced to two-cars by removing the unpowered centre cars, causing horrendous overcrowding - but it also led to some exciting runs with 720hp 2-car units! For a time, passengers even had to endure the use of Pacer railbuses whose 4-wheel coaches and bus-type seats were totally unsuitable and rode very badly on the route's curves and gradients. The Calder Valley DMUs bowed out in 1987 as the Class 150/2 Sprinters took over. Ten years later, services were worked by a mixture of Super Sprinters and air conditioned Class 158s.

Freight

It is no over-statement to say that Calderdale's industrial expansion could not have happened without the railways. Only they with their spectacular and expensive civil engineering masterpieces could penetrate the rugged Pennine landscape to serve all parts.

Traffic connected with Calderdale's traditional industries - textiles and the manufacture of carpets, machine tools, wire and toffee dominated and the railways built warehouses for storing and distributing wool, shoddy rags and cotton. On the main line ran a succession of trains taking coal from pits east of the Pennines to industry and coal shipping ports in Lancashire.

In the 1950s more than half Britain's freight went by rail and the Calder Valley was a freight artery. In 1960 a goods train was booked over Hall Royd Junction, Todmorden, on average every 17 minutes in one direction or another, hauled almost exclusively by the unlovely but sturdy WD 2-8-0s. Some were through coal trains from places like Normanton, Crofton and Mirfield, or big pits like Carlton Main near Barnsley, but much of the coal came to Mytholmroyd sidings. There, trains were split and the wagons sorted into fresh trains according to their destinations. Some took the main line to the Manchester and Liverpool areas, and others the slog over Copy Pit to the yards at Rose Grove where they were re-sorted. As in more recent times, the empties mostly went back to Healey Mills. Express and mixed goods trains of various kinds added some variety.

From the 1960s, freight traffic declined rapidly and by the mid-1980s it consisted mainly of petroleum products, including trains from the Shell refinery at Stanlow, Cheshire, to Leeds

Typical Calder Valley freight - WD 2-8-0 No. 90408 passes Summit East signal box on its way up to Summit Tunnel with a westbound Through Freight composed of coal wagons at 1.37pm on 18th August, 1962. (*Robert Anderson*)

which in steam days brought double-headed Birkenhead-based 9F 2-10-0s to Yorkshire.

In August, 1985 BR declared the Calder Valley its main cross-Pennine freight route because easier gradients allowed heavier loads than the LNW line through Huddersfield. As a result, 1,100-tonne block coal trains between Yorkshire and Fiddlers Ferry power station, near Warrington, were switched from the LNW line and once again the Calder Valley reverberated to the sound of heavy loaded coal trains going west and empty wagons returning east. Freight continued at a fairly high level during the late 1980s but collapsed altogether in the 1990s. The use of coal imported through Liverpool meant that by 1997 the "Fiddlers" were running only spasmodically, while several oil terminals on both sides of the Pennines had closed - including the Shell terminal in Leeds - all but eliminating the familiar tank trains. Some new traffic started in 1996/7 but it remains minimal and is a sad reflection of the railway's decline as a freight carrier.

All change

In the late 19th Century freight in the Calder Valley was so heavy that it played havoc with passenger trains - doing nothing to help the L&Y's reputation for poor service to passengers - and between the late 1880s and 1920s the line was progressively quadrupled where possible with loops and refuge sidings added elsewhere. A number of stations had to be rebuilt to take

account of the widening and Mytholmroyd yard opened in 1919.

But no sooner had the 20th Century dawned than local passenger services came under pressure from a growing network of electric trams offering a cheaper and more convenient alternative, as did the buses that followed from the 1920s, and rail patronage plummetted.

The Halifax High Level was the first casualty, its passenger trains axed in 1917 as a wartime economy but not reinstated afterwards. When the trams reached Stainland and Ripponden the L&Y reacted in 1907 by introducing more economical steam railmotor services. It opened new halts on the Rishworth branch at Sowerby Bridge station and Watson Crossing, and on the Stainland branch at Greetland Rochdale Road. This failed to stop the rot but the railway had a trump card. The LMS was a partner in the Halifax Joint Omnibus Committee and in 1929 it replaced the Stainland and Rishworth trains with what were effectively its own buses doing the same to the trams that they did to the trains.

Another tram and bus victim, Dewsbury Market Place, closed on 30th November, 1930. The very last passenger train was a rugby league special arriving back from Hull just after 11pm.

Local passenger trains over the Pickle Bridge line went in September, 1931. Then in 1948 the worsening state of Wyke Viaduct forced BR to reroute all remaining passenger trains, the line closing completely in 1952. Half of the viaduct was eventually demolished leaving the remainder a somewhat bizarre landmark visible in 1997 from Halifax-Bradford trains.

Serious modernisation began in 1932 when the LMS installed an American-style speed signalling system on the complex section through Mirfield. It featured searchlight signals showing various combinations of green, yellow and red to instruct drivers on what speeds they should observe as well as whether they should stop, proceed or run at caution.

Despite losing many of their passengers to trams and buses the Queensbury lines hung on until 1955. Then, with Queensbury Tunnel needing £70,000 worth of repairs and unconfirmed reports that the six Halifax-Bradford, five Bradford-Halifax, two Keighley-Halifax and one Halifax-Keighley trains were used by only 27 passengers a day, BR axed the service on 23rd May. The passenger stations were kept for excursion traffic but Holmfield-Queensbury closed completely in May, 1956.

Next to go were the Bradford-Thornhill trains, withdrawn at the end of 1957, and the Bradford/Halifax-Wakefield, Normanton/ Goole service in 1962.

BR's policy of concentrating goods traffic on a few central depots spelt the end for most Calderdale branch lines which had survived to carry freight. The Rishworth branch, cut back to Ripponden in 1953, shut completely in 1958, the Stainland branch going a year later.

General goods was already being dealt with by road vans from Sowerby Bridge and coal traffic was switched there as well.

The end came for the Halifax and Ovenden andthe Halifax High Level in June, 1960 when, despite protests from 22 coal merchants, BR closed the lines from North Bridge to Holmfield and St. Paul's, coal business moving to Halifax Church Street and North Bridge depots. By then the number of Halifax-Holmfield-St. Paul's goods trains had dropped from three a day to three a week. North Bridge depot stayed in business until 1st April, 1974.

Dewsbury Market Place was wiped out in February, 1961 when freight facilities were concentrated on the ex-GN Railway Street depot. Four years later, the Market Place branch was revived when the closed Headfield spur to the nearby GN line was reinstated so that Railway Street could be served direct from Healey Mills. Railway Street closed in 1990 but a portion of the branch survives in 1998 to serve a cement depot on the site of the wagon works.

The newly modernised Healey Mills yard, designed to handle 4,000 wagons a day, opened in July, 1963, replacing smaller yards like Mytholmroyd, Brighouse and Mirfield. Healey Mills diesel depot was completed in March, 1966, ultimately rendering Mirfield and other steam depots redundant. Sowerby Bridge shed had already closed.

DMUs took over most Bradford-Huddersfield

Steam and seaside excursion trains were destined to disappear and Easter Monday, 1966 was something of a swansong for both. The morning saw five Jubilee-hauled excursions go over Copy Pit including this one, the 8.48am Bradford to Blackpool being hauled confidently away from Stansfield Hall by the pride of Low Moor shed, No. 45565 *Victoria. (Robert Anderson)*

trains in November, 1959 but the economies they brought could not save them from the Beeching axe. All passenger trains via Heckmondwike and stopping services via Halifax were withdrawn on 14th June, 1965 and the Heckmondwike-Mirfield stretch closed completely. The surviving Bradford-Stockport service of one daily DMU and steam train each way, was withdrawn on 5th November, 1966.

Todmorden felt Beeching's axe in 1965 when its local service over Copy Pit to East Lancashire was withdrawn and again the following year when the Todmorden-Manchester stopping trains were taken off.

Closure of the LNW "New Line" in 1966 saw more Trans-Pennine trains routed through Mirfield, while a new spur had to be laid from the Spen Valley line at Heckmondwike so that oil trains could reach a terminal on the "New Line" at Liversedge Spen.

By this time there were few railways left to close in Calderdale although the Low Moor-Thornhill line was severed for three and a half years while the M62 motorway was built across its path. It reopened in 1974 but the freight decline in Halifax and Bradford rendered it superfluous and it closed in 1981. The Thornhill-Liversedge Spen section remained for a few years but has since been lifted. The Low Moor-Cleckheaton portion survived, buried under weeds for eventual use as an electric tramway carrying vintage trams from the Transperience transport museum on the site of Low Moor goods yard. Alas, the three year-old museum, built with public money, ran into financial difficulties in 1997 and the Cleckheaton line's future looks bleak.

The late 1960s/early 70s saw the main line extensively rationalised. Signalling between Elland and Healey Mills was fully modernised with multiple aspect colour lights, track circuits, train describers and brought under the control of the new power signal box at Healey Mills. Running lines were reduced to two in most places and the "New Line" underpass at Heaton Lodge reopened as a flyunder to keep Trans-Pennine expresses clear of Calder Valley freight, helping relieve congestion created when the "New Line" closed. Commissioned over the weekend 25-27th April, 1970, this scheme also replaced the speed signalling. The Eastwood-Littleborough section and the Copy Pit line were modernised and brought under the control of a new power signal box at Preston by 1975. Again, track was rationalised and the Stansfield Hall-Todmorden section of the Copy Pit line, closed since March, 1973, was severed. Semaphore signalling remained between Hebden Bridge and Elland but the number of boxes was steadily reduced. Signalling was also progressively rationalised between Milner Royd and Bradford to the point where in 1998 there were only five signal boxes in the whole of Calderdale: Hebden Bridge, Milner Royd, Halifax East, Elland, and Greetland No. 2 which is normally switched out of use. A crazy 1980s plan to single the Halifax-Bradford section fortunately came to nothing.

On Monday 3rd October, 1988 a lorry hit a bridge on the LNW line at Mossley, forcing Trans-Pennine expresses on to the Calder Valley for most of the day. Class 47 No. 47488 *Railriders* races past Hebden Bridge and one of the few remaining Calderdale signal boxes with the 14.20 Newcastle-Liverpool. *(Stephen Chapman)*

The late 1980s rerouting of Calderdale's last summer Saturday services spelt complete closure for the Greetland-Dryclough and Bradley Wood curves, and of the Greetland-Bradley Wood section of the main line, to regular passenger traffic. Diverted Trans-Pennine passenger trains still use the main line but the curves are mothballed.

The Calder Valley main line has faced two serious closure threats, neither of them during the Beeching era. In fact, Dr. Beeching wanted to turn it into the premier Trans-Pennine route seeing it as having potential for higher speeds than the line through Huddersfield but this did not happen. In the late 1970s BR discovered over-capacity on its four trans-Pennine routes and considered closing two of them. For a time, the L&Y faced a real threat of closure west of Halifax but in the end BR opted to shut only the electrified and by then freight only Manchester-Sheffield Woodhead line, rerouting much of its traffic, mostly the Fiddler's Ferry coal trains, via Healey Mills. The second closure threat followed a monumental catastrophe that went down in railway folklore. At about 5.30am on 20th December, 1984 the Haverton Hill to Glazebrook petrol train derailed deep inside Summit Tunnel. Some of the thirteen 100 ton tankers were punctured and their contents set alight. After burning for several hours the train exploded like a volcano. Flames shot 300ft up the ventilation shafts and another 200ft into the air above ground. The tunnel became a raging furnace, melting and twisting the train and the track beneath it, and vitrifying and spalling 400 yards of the 140 year-old brick lining.

Nothing could survive such an inferno - so everyone thought. The expense of repairing such damage would be too much for BR. It seemed inevitable that the tunnel would stay closed. For a week no-one, not even BR engineers, were allowed near the tunnel which was put under police guard. When it was cool and safe enough for them to go inside and inspect the damage - under fire brigade escort - they got quite a shock. They emerged gushing tributes to George Stephenson and his colleagues and announced that the tunnel could and would be repaired.

BR's willingness to spend £1.5 million on the tunnel was seen as a great vote of confidence in the line and the reopening eight months later was the cause of much celebration.

Meanwhile, things had been happening on the Copy Pit line which by the early 1980s had no trains at all on most weekdays - only an empty Blackburn-Hall Royd DMU to keep the rails clean so that the track circuits would operate safely. BR considered closing the line but then came the merger of the Bradford-based National Provincial and the Burnley building societies. Burnley staff were transferred to the N&P headquarters in Bradford and the society guaranteed BR a certain number of season tickets if it would lay on a daily train for them. A Preston-Bradford DMU started running on 14th May, 1984 but the following October BR introduced five more Leeds-Preston trains each way. This has since blossomed into an hourly York/Scarborough-Blackpool service forming part of the successful Trans-Pennine Express network operated by Class 158 units.

A renaissance of all West Yorkshire's passenger rail network began in the early 1970s following several depressing post-Beeching years during which patronage slumped. A BR marketing drive in 1972 turned an annual five per cent loss of passengers into a five per cent increase. West Yorkshire routes were given brand names, Leeds-Halifax-Manchester becoming the Caldervale Line.

In 1976 the West Yorkshire Passenger Transport Executive became responsible for the county's public transport and since then it has led an incredible revival of rail's fortunes. Competitive fares, imaginative multi-journey and pre-paid tickets and more attractive timetables have attracted passengers back in millions. According to PTE figures, 2.6 million passengers used the Leeds-Todmorden section of the Caldervale line in 1985/6 though most would be between Leeds, Bradford and Halifax. By 1997 the number of passengers travelling on the MetroTrain network as the whole West Yorkshire system had been branded, had reached a record 16 million.

Since 1987 ways of restoring lost portions of Calderdale's railway have been examined in a bid to reduce road traffic. These have included reinstating the Todmorden triangle and reopening a whole host of stations but 10 years later only Walsden, between Todmorden and Summit Tunnel, has reopened although the existing ones have been refurbished.

One scheme which might actually go ahead is the reinstatement by 2000 of a Halifax-Huddersfield service using the mothballed Dryclough-Greetland and Bradley Wood curves, serving reopened Elland and Brighouse stations and bringing back a worthwhile chunk of Calderdale's lost railway.

Black Five 4-6-0 No. 44895 is about to enter the inky blackness of Summit Tunnel with the 11.15 Scarborough-Liverpool Exchange on 18th August, 1962 *(Robert Anderson)* When the tunnel and the completed line opened on 1st March, 1841, the first passengers must have thought they were being taken straight to Hell as they plunged in open wagons into the depths of the unknown, 300ft below ground, in total darkness, their ears assailed by a deafening racket and their heads showered with smoke and sparks.

THE MAIN LINE & ITS BRANCHES

Below: Carlisle-based Jubilee No.45716 *Swiftsure* beats a path towards Summit Tunnel with the 11.32 Scarborough-Manchester express on 25th August, 1962. *(Robert Anderson)*

SHORT MEMORIES

20.9.52: A1/1 Pacific 60113 *Great Northern* powers the Northern Rubber Co.'s annual Retford-Blackpool illuminations excursion over Copy Pit.

February, 1953: Royal Scot 4-6-0s 46131 *The Royal Warwickshire Regiment,* 46144 *Honourable Artillery Company* and 46146 *The Rifle Brigade* haul three trainloads of Arsenal football supporters from London to Burnley via Manchester, Todmorden and Copy Pit.

July, 1953: V2 2-6-2 60865 takes a York to Liverpool express as far as Todmorden where it is replaced by a "Crab" 2-6-0.

Above: Class D11/1 "Director" 4-4-0s Nos. 62664 *Princess Mary* and 62662 *Prince of Wales* coast down from Summit Tunnel towards Walsden with the Ian Allan "Pennine Pullman" railtour of 12th May, 1956. The train travelled from London via Sheffield to Manchester, returning via the Calder Valley and Barnsley.

Below: Shortly to become the last standard gauge steam locomotive to work for British Rail, Britannia Pacific No. 70013 *Oliver Cromwell* passes the site of Walsden station, closed in 1961, with a Manchester-bound special in July, 1968.
The level crossing was abolished a few years later and today a new station stands where No. 70013 is passing. *(Peter Wood)*

17

Above: How the west end of Todmorden station looked in 1962 when Jubilee No. 45710 *Irresistible* was calling there with a Manchester Victoria express. Behind the locomotive is the coal yard that is now the station car park while the mass of Stoodley Pike dominates the right background. *(Peter Wood)*

This is the third Todmorden station on this spot and dates from 1881.

Left: Situated on the Down side opposite the goods yard was Todmorden West signal box, closed on 10th January, 1965. *(Peter Wood)*

Right: At the west end of Todmorden in early 1964 with a single car diesel parcels unit approaching the cotton warehouse and Dob Royd level crossing while returning to Manchester. Cranes and furniture containers complete a busy goods yard scene. *(Peter Wood)*

Above: Todmorden Up side goods yard was still busy with coal on 14th June, 1968 when, with the end of the steam age in sight, Rose Grove 8F 2-8-0 No. 48410 was doing the shunting. *(Peter Rose)*

Right: One of the antiquated and awkward mobile hand cranes used to unload goods at Todmorden since L&Y days. *(Peter Wood)*

Back in 1956 Todmorden station was equipped to handle general goods, parcels, furniture vans, carriages, motor cars, portable engines, machines on wheels, livestock, horse boxes, prize cattle vans, wagonload coals and minerals, and carriages and motor cars by passenger and parcels train. It had yard cranes capable of lifting up to 10 tons maximum and there was one private siding - Fielden's Siding which served the Waterside Mill via an elevated track running from the siding at Dob Royd and over the Rochdale canal to the mill. Todmorden closed to goods traffic on 2nd November, 1964 but continued to receive coal until 2nd October, 1972, and handled parcels until well into the 1980s.

Demolition of the Down side warehouse opened up this view showing Hull B1 4-6-0 No. 61306 on one of Todmorden's several daily parcels trains. The through siding used for stabling coaches overnight is in the foreground, the garden just in front of the nearest platform canopy and the station master's house behind the engine. 61306 was later transferred to Low Moor where it became the last of 410 B1s when withdrawn in October, 1967. It is preserved for all to see today. *(Peter Wood)*

Jack Storah worked at Todmorden for the best part of 35 years, spending the first six years from 1956 in the goods yard:

"It was a busy yard then. We used the yard crane for unloading standard furniture-type containers, they were heavy and it was hard to operate. It had two handles and needed three people on each so everyone had to help, clerks included.

"In the cotton warehouse we had to use a nasty little crane which was squat over a hole in the floor. Cotton bales, from America and Egypt, weighed two or three hundredweight each and needed a lot of effort to lift. Again, everyone had to muck in. Once the crane handle flew back and hit one of the yard checkers in the mouth, knocking out all but one of his front teeth. The cotton was distributed to mills all around Todmorden.

"We received horses and cattle in vans detached from freight and passenger trains at the cattle dock which was later used for loading scrap metal.

"The worst things we handled were stinking, sweating sacks of raw wool going to Bradford after sheep shearing.

"Once a week a barrel of beer came rom Burton-on-Trent for a pub called The Grapes, and carboys of bromine from Cornwall for making photographic chemicals."

The Queen Hotel opposite the station had an upstairs bar connected to the Up platform by a covered footbridge over the station road.

"We called it Queen Top. I think the bridge was removed in the 1960s after being boarded up for some time."

When a wagon of coal came for Todmorden East signal box, the paperwork illustrated the kind of bureaucracy on the railway then.

"So much coal could not be emptied on the day it arrived so we had to raise a coal merchant's demurrage charge, send it to Manchester and they marked it 'no charge'. We did that for all internal traffic because everything had to be accounted for."

Jack faced more form filling when he moved to parcels and booking office duties in the 1960s.

"On market day we got 20 to 30 boxes of fish from Grimsby and Hull. The fish merchants came from the market to collect them and if you were lucky you got some to take home. Every box was numbered and had an invoice, and every one had to be marked off in the 'fish book.' The empties had to go back and if one was missing someone would be on the phone wanting to know where it was.

"There were three of us then, we did a few weeks in the booking office and two or three in the parcels office. A porter was on duty all night because we handled parcels around the clock.

"Regular parcels for despatch included castings from a local engineering firm and Venetian blinds made in Walsden. Our van driver often needed two trips to bring them down and we could have 300 stood on end around the office walls."

Day old chicks in their cardboard containers were a regular commodity: "We called it the 'chicken train' - a daily Bradford to Manchester parcels which picked up the chickens. Thornbers who supplied the whole country with chickens, had their own platform at Mytholmroyd. At Todmorden Finney's of Lob Mill were the main consignor."

Homing pigeons being sent away for a race back to Todmorden were a familiar sight too: "We especially got a lot on Friday nights. If there was a race on there were 20-30 baskets to Macclesfield, Chelford or Moston which were all in a straight line from Todmorden.

"At holiday times we needed extra booking office staff and passengers would be queuing down the road. Holiday trains ran to Torquay, Portsmouth & Southsea, Blackpool and Southport and an overnight train went to London, although their exact destinations varied each summer."

Todmorden was not an easy place to handle parcels. With no goods lift, getting them from one platform to the other meant lugging them down off one platform, across the track and back up onto the other. An indicator on one of the platform canopy supports showed when it was safe to perform this backbreaking task.

"It was alright when there were plenty of us but from the 1970s when we handled only Red Star parcels the staff was reduced to one man and the job became impossible, especially when you got castings weighing 2cwt."

Stripped to the bare essentials years ago, the

Evidence of Todmorden's trade in poultry. This brass hamper plate was unearthed in the publisher's garden.

station was once a very different place: "We had first class and ladies' waiting rooms, with coal fires, and until about the early 1950s, a bookstall on the Up platform."

Todmorden was famous for its prize-winning gardens and cast concrete BR lion and wheel emblems: "There was a lion and wheel on the Leeds platform and one at Hall Royd. A p way man called O'Neil did them and they were painted in the correct colours. The gardens on the Leeds platform included a fountain and a little waterfall, and there was a fish tank on the Manchester side."

TODMORDEN DEPARTURES(MON-FRI) SUMMER 1961

Down direction

5.14am	4.20 Manchester Vic.-Normanton
7.7am	6.15 Manchester Vic.-Bradford
7.38am	6.5 Manchester Vic.-Normanton
8.48am	8.8 Manchester Vic.-Bradford/Leeds
9.49am	9.5 Manchester Vic.-Wakefield Kirkgate
10.3am	8.3 Liverpool Exch.-Bradford/Leeds
10.53am	10.15 Manchester Vic.-York
11.10am	9.40 Liverpool Exch.-Bradford/Leeds
1.2pm	11.30am Liverpool Exch.-Bradford/Leeds
2.2pm	12.30 Liverpool Exch.-Bradford
4.5pm	2.30 Liverpool Exch-Bradford/Leeds
5.6pm	3.30 Liverpool Exch.-Bradford/Leeds
5.23pm	4.37 Manchester Vic-Halifax
5.49pm	5.10 Manchester Vic-York
6.2pm	4.30 Liverpool Exch.-Bradford/Leeds
6.20pm	To Halifax
6.46pm	5.57 Manchester Vic-Normanton
8.3pm	6.30 Liverpool Exch.-York
9.18pm	To Preston
10.22pm	8.30 Liverpool Exch.-Bradford/Leeds

Up direction

4.39am	3.36 Leeds-Manchester Vic
4.54am	2.8 York-Manchester Vic.
7.30am	6.32 Bradford-Liverpool Exch.
7.51am	To Manchester Victoria
8.13am	7.15 Bradford-Manchester Vic.
8.32am	6.30 Normanton-Manchester Vic.
9.8am	To Burnley and Preston
10am	8.25 Leeds/8.45 Bradford-Liverpool
10.19am	8.50 Normanton-Manchester Vic
10.20am	To Burnley and Preston
11.18am	To Burnley and Preston
11.47am	10.10 York-Manchester Vic.
12.4pm	10.55 Leeds/11.13 Bradford-Liverpool Exch
12.18pm	To Burnley and Preston
1.20pm	12.0 Wakefield Kirkgate-Manchester Vic
2.7pm	12.55 Leeds/1.15 Bradford-Liverpool Exch.
2.18pm	To Burnley and Preston
3.42pm	2.2pm York-Liverpool Exch.
4.18pm	To Burnley and Preston
5.14pm	4.42 Halifax-Manchester Vic.
6.13pm	5.10 Leeds/5.15 Bradford-Liverpool Exch.
6.18pm	To Burnley and Preston
7.12pm	5.23 York-Manchester Vic.
7.53pm	6.30 Wakefield Kirkgate-Manchester Vic.
8.12pm	6.55 Leeds/7.15 Bradford-Southport
8.45pmFO	7.50 Wakefield Kirkgate-Liverpool Exch.
8.55pm	7.9 York-Liverpool Exch.
10.21pm	8.55 Leeds-Manchester Vic.
10.55pm SO	To Burnley and Accrington

Above: Fairburn 2-6-4T No. 42110 appeared to be facing the wrong way when waiting to leave Todmorden's Burnley bay platform with the 9.10pm for Manchester Victoria on 3rd June, 1960. In fact, at that time the train ran via Burnley, Accrington and Bury.

This scene is barely recognisable in 1998. The warehouse long demolished, the bay abandoned and the space filled in, and the platform considerably shortened and fenced off. *(Robert Anderson)*

Below: A flashback to the days of the Lancashire and Yorkshire Railway. On the left, looking towards Manchester, are the Burnley bay and grain warehouse, the main line platforms are centre, and on the right the Down side warehouse and three-way splitting signal controlling entrance to the Down Goods line and the line to Copy Pit as well as the main line. On the hill is Dobroyd Castle, home of the Fieldens, a prominent local family. *(Lens of Sutton)*

No book on Calderdale's railways would be complete without mentioning Todmorden's buses.

As in Halifax, they were partly run by the railway - the LMS being a partner in the Todmorden Joint Omnibus Committee.

The once-familiar Leyland double deckers with the LMS crest on their sides had to be a low bridge variety, otherwise they would not fit in the town's bus garage.

To achieve the low profile, the top deck seats were all to one side with the gangway in a well along the other. Lower deck passengers had to watch their heads as the gangway well protruded below the lower deck ceiling.

Todmorden buses were renowned for their spotless condition inside and out.

In 1997, two present-day buses, one double and one single deck, still carried the TJOC green and cream livery.

Above: With less than two months to go before the end of BR steam, Black Five 4-6-0 No. 44735 heads the 07.50 Middleton Junction to Healey Mills empties over Todmorden viaduct on 14th June, 1968. In the background, the grain warehouse at the station had by this time been demolished.

Down below is Burnley Road and the town's bus station. Nowadays, the town centre is ravaged by heavy traffic which includes huge 12-wheel juggernaut lorries while only a handful of freight trains run each day *(Peter Rose)*

Below: Todmorden buses line up in Millwood garage, Halifax Road. As in Halifax, the LMS was a partner in the Todmorden Joint Omnibus Committee. *(Jack Wild)*

Above: With the steep Todmorden Edge looming above, Carlisle Kingmoor Jubilee No. 45678 *De Robeck* approaches Hall Royd with an eastbound stopping passenger train on 30th September, 1961. The goods lines on the left, the semaphore signals, signal boxes like Todmorden East in the distance, and the west side of the triangle were all removed in the 1970s but the sidings on the right were kept for engineers' use. They remained in 1997, disused and disappearing under weeds and bushes. *(P.B.Booth/N.E.Stead collection)*

Above: An Accrington-based Cravens diesel multiple unit rounds the curve from Stansfield Hall to Todmorden station with a local from Preston shortly before the service was axed in 1965. The L&Y opened a station here in 1869 so that expresses travelling direct between Yorkshire and East Lancashire could serve Todmorden. The station closed in 1944 and by the 1960s only a space remained where the platforms used to be. *(Peter Wood)*

Until 28th June, 1975, locomotives were allowed to work "wrong line" over the Down Goods between Hall Royd and Todmorden, while up to 20 loaded or 30 empty wagons could be worked without a brake van between Hall Royd and Stansfield Hall.

Above: Enthusiasts pay homage to the Copy Pit banker which on 14th June, 1968 was 8F No. 48493 of Rose Grove shed, topping up with water in the engine siding adjoining the since abandoned Todmorden East-Stansfield Hall curve. Todmorden East signal box is in the distance. *(Peter Rose)*
By 1998 this area was a mass of trees and scrub but the Todmorden Steam Centre Trust aims to build an engine shed here for maintaining preserved main line steam locos. So far, it has an exhibition in the old parcels office at the station where a model of the proposed shed can be seen.

LOCOMOTIVES ASSISTING IN REAR OF TRAINS TO COPY PIT: In clear weather freight trains need not come to a stand, but the driver must reduce speed to allow the assisting locomotive to reach the train as soon as possible. *L.M. Region Northern Area Sectional Appendix, 1977.*

On 14th June, 1968 Peter Rose and two friends were among those witnessing some of the country's last main line steam trains at Todmorden.

First they saw the Copy Pit banker, 8F 2-8-0 No.48493, return to Stansfield Hall and crossover to refill at the water column. Then...

"Some detective work with the freight working timetable produced timings for two steam freights. We made our way to the station for the first, the 07.50 Middleton Junction to Healey Mills. But there, we found 48410 simmering in the goods yard before making its last shunt.

We thought our cup was running over when the Middleton came as planned, Class 5 4-6-0 44735 wheeling its train through at fair speed. Our part morning ended triumphantly with the 06.46 Farrington to Healey Mills coming off the Copy Pit line."

Right: No. 48493 returns from Copy Pit and passes Stansfield Hall signal box while on its way to take water. Part of the line to Todmorden East on the extreme right survives in 1998 as a single track loco siding should it ever be needed. *(Peter Rose)*

Left: The end of steam is nigh but there is still a job to do. The Copy Pit banker, an 8F 2-8-0, shoves a heavy coal train hauled by another 8F up the tortuous 1 in 65 past Mons Mill, Todmorden. *(Peter Wood)*

On 5th December, 1904 there was a spectacular pile-up when two engines were chased down from Copy Pit by their own train.

About 40 wagons of a Rose Grove-Wakefield goods broke loose on the 1 in 65 descent. The loco crews accelerated their engines and remaining 10 wagons but the runaways caught them up at Stansfield Hall station.

The July, 1905 Railway Magazine reported: "Many wagons were knocked to matchwood...goods flew in all directions. The platform was heaped with wreckage and the station lamps levelled...The impact was heard all over Todmorden." Nobody was seriously hurt.

A crash at Cornholme during the night of 15th August, 1967 had more tragic results.

The driver of Type 4 diesel D398 died when his Lostock Hall-Healey Mills train of 36 loaded vans and empty mineral wagons crashed into the Copy Pit banker, an 8F 2-8-0, at an estimated 60-70mph. Wreckage was flung over a mile of track, several wagons rolling down an embankment severely damaging lineside property.

Below: Some of the last standard gauge steam trains operated by British Rail ran through the Calder Valley and this was one of the very last, on the last day of true steam working. On 4th August, 1968 Black Fives 44871 and 45017 storm the 1 in 65 climb up through Cornholme and towards Copy Pit with a Birmingham - Carlisle "Farewell to Steam" railtour. *(Peter Wood)*

Right: Climbing from Stansfield Hall to Copy Pit, the first station was Cornholme, pictured here in the early 1900s. The passenger-only station closed in September, 1938 and little remains to be seen in 1998, the best pointer being Station Road, just off the Burnley Road.
(Lens of Sutton)

Below: Portsmouth station also in the early 1900s. It stayed open for passengers until 7th July, 1958 and to goods until 15th July, 1963. No trace remains in 1998, however, except for the level crossing which is operated by road users.
(Lens of Sutton)

Bottom: Having just thrashed its way through closed Portsmouth station, Black Five No. 44694 has about a mile to go up the 1 in 80 to Copy Pit Summit where it will reach 749ft above sea level. Heading the 8.2am Bradford to Blackpool excursion on Whit Monday, 30th May, 1966, it is crossing what is now the Yorkshire/ Lancashire border.
(Robert Anderson)

Above: The bridge at Hall Royd has long been a popular vantage point for photographers. This was the view on 30th September, 1961 as Wakefield-based WD 2-8-0 No. 90100 comes off the Copy Pit line with an eastbound train of empty loose-coupled wagons.

Below: When the world's fastest steam locomotive came to the Calder Valley. Class A4 4-6-2 No. 60022 *Mallard* takes the Copy Pit line at Hall Royd with the Northern Rubber Company's annual outing from Retford to the Blackpool illuminations on the same day as the above photo. A WD banker supposed to help the train up from Stansfield Hall was left standing by *Mallard*.
Even though the train returned at two in the morning, people lined the route to see the 126mph record breaker come back, double headed as far as Stansfield Hall with ex-Midland Railway Compound 4-4-0 No. 1000. *(Both P. B. Booth / N. E. Stead collection)*

Shortly after 3pm on 21st June, 1912 a Liverpool to Leeds and Bradford express was derailed at 45mph on the tight curve built to avoid the aborted tunnel at Charlestown.

Six people died but considering the devastation it is amazing the toll was not higher.

The train consisted of an L&Y 2-4-2T and seven coaches plus a 6-wheel van carrying a coffin placed between the first two coaches, contrary to normal practice. The second coach was wrecked with the third tipped on its side.

Local people rushed to the rescue, tearing up their own bedsheets for bandages and using carriage doors for stretchers.

The positioning of the 6-wheeled van is thought to have been the main factor causing the crash. It should have been at the back but was brought forward because the last three coaches were going to Bradford.

The 2-4-2Ts were subsequently not used on such expresses and the main line was relaid on a straighter alignment, the abandoned curve still visible to this day.

Above: A Caprotti Black Five 4-6-0 races an early 1960s eastbound express past the remains of Eastwood station between Todmorden and Hebden Bridge.
Eastwood had very low, short timber platforms and passengers from Halifax had to travel in the front two coaches. A box ladder was provided for getting off the train. The station closed to passengers on 3rd December, 1951 but continued to receive coal until 18th May, 1964. *(Peter Wood)*

Below: Having just passed Charlestown, Low Moor's celebrity Jubilee No. 45565 *Victoria* races the 10.10 Bradford-Blackpool excursion towards Eastwood on Whit. Monday, 1966.
This view has changed dramatically since then. The loops have gone, the last lifted after being damaged by a coal train derailment in 1989, and the whole scene is obscured by trees encroaching on the two remaining main lines. *(Robert Anderson).*

Above: Between 1965 and 1967 *Victoria*, kept spotless by enthusiasts, was a regular sight on Blackpool trains. Here she is bringing the last run of the 1.25pm Blackpool to Leeds and Bradford past Hebden Bridge goods yard and into the station on 27th August, 1966. *(Robert Anderson)*

In 1956, Hebden Bridge was equipped to handle all kinds of goods and had a 10 ton yard crane while a private siding served the gas works. Goods facillities were withdrawn on 2nd May, 1966 and the goods yard is now the station car park.

Hebden Bridge miraculously survived the years of rationalisation when everything but the bare essentials was stripped away from most stations. With platform canopies, L&Y signs and parcels lift all intact, it was fully restored in the late 1970s after which it won several awards. In 1997 the station was extensively renovated again with all its traditional features still preserved.

Below: Looking west in the early 1980s with one of the "Calder Valley" Class 110 DMUs reduced to two-cars. *(Fastline Photographic)*

SHORT MEMORIES

November, 1955: A football special runs from Halifax to Bradford via the Queensbury line, closed to passengers last May.

7.6.57: An experimental diesel electric multiple unit converted from two passenger coaches completes a week of Bradford-Liverpool test runs via Halifax. More Halifax-Todmorden-Bradford-Huddersfield tests are run in October.

Summer 1957: 9F 2-10-0s working summer Saturday passenger trains like the 2.20pm Blackpool-Sheffield on 10th and 17th August.

August, 1957: Thieves blow the safe at Elland station and steal the takings.

14.9.57: Seven B1s noted on Blackpool illuminations specials.

Right: Looking down on Hebden Bridge in the early 1900s with the east end on the right and the west end on the left. Buildings long since disappeared include the large mill right of the station and the big goods warehouse with its yard full of wagons on the left.
(Lens of Sutton)

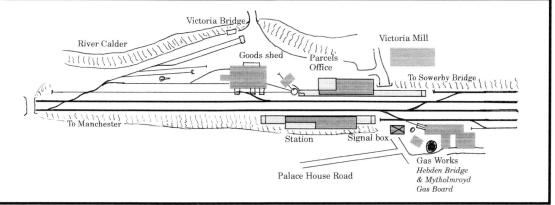

When..it is necessary to run Down trains with wagons to detach at Hebden Bridge into the Slow line...the signalman will advise the Shunter who will instruct drivers. When no Shunter is on duty, drivers must be alert for a hand signal to draw up before detaching. *BR NE Region Sectional Appendix, 1960.*

Above: Hebden Bridge in 1921. (*Not to scale***)**

Below: Mytholmroyd in 1965 with a Liverpool-Harrogate "Calder Valley" DMU passing through. The station was de-staffed in 1985 and the wooden buildings on the left have gone. *(Jack Wild)*

Above: Mytholmroyd sorting sidings on 1st August, 1963 as a WD 2-8-0 arrives with a load of coal from Horbury. Shunting went on here round the clock except on Saturday afternoons and Sundays. The 45 year-old yard closed in January, 1964 following completion of the big marshalling yard at Healey Mills. *(Jack Wild/Stephen Chapman collection)*

▄■ FREIGHT TRAINS STARTING AND TERMINATING AT MYTHOLMROYD ■▄
2nd November, 1959 - 12th June, 1960

Time		Train
12.40am	MX	Class J to Bury Knowsely Street
3.20am	MX	12.55am class H from Wakefield
3.15am	MO	Class J to Manchester Ship Canal
4.54am		4.5am class J from Laisterdyke
5am	MO	Class J to Royton Junction
5.20am	MX	Class J to Royton Junction
5.21am	MX	3.50am class J from Carlton North
5.40am	MO	Class J to Rose Grove
6.7am	MO	4.50am class H from Normanton
7am		Class K to Hebden Bridge
7.58am	MX	4am class K from Normanton
8.55am	MSX	Class J to Royton Jn.*(suspended)*
9.16am	MX	To Royton Junction
10.25am		Class J to Moston*(Aintree SO)*
10.48am	MX	9.10am class K from Brighouse
10.57am	SX	Class J to Fazakerley
10.57am	SO	Class J to Moston
11.7am		9am class J from Carlton
11.20am	MSX	Light engine to Newton Heath
		(off 9.10 from Brighouse)
11.35am	SO	Light engine to Rose Grove
		(off 9.10 from Brighouse)
12.4pm	MSX	Class J to Manchester Ship Canal
12.5pm	SO	8am class K from Normanton
12.25pm	SX	Class J to Ramsbottom

Time		Train
12.25pm	SO	Class K to Bury Knowsely Street
12.45pm	SX	Class J to Rose Grove*(12.50 SO)*
1.15pm	SO	Class K to Hebden Bridge
2.15pm	SO	11am class K from Dewsbury Market Place
2.40pm	SX	11.40am class K from Dewsbury MP
3.17pm	SX	1.20pm class K from Normanton
4.15pm	SO	Class J to Manchester Ship Canal
5.15pm	MSX	Class J to Fazakerley*(suspended)*
5.41pm		Class J from Carlton
6.1pm	SX	Class J from Crigglestone East
7pm	SX	Class H to Moston
7.10pm	SX	5.30pm class H from Crofton South
8.22pm	SO	6.50pm class J from Laisterdyke
8.52pm	SX	8.30pm class F from Halifax
9.10pm	SX	Class J to Rose Grove
9.14pm	SO	8.5pm Class H from Wakefield

All trains were in the Up direction with a small number of light engine movements in the Down direction. Numerous light engines ran from Sowerby Bridge motive power depot to Mytholmroyd to work the various trains originating there. The 6.50pm SX Hillhouse-Aintree class H was one through train which stopped at Mytholmroyd to change engines.

In the Down direction most mineral trains, mainly empties from Lancashire, ran to Healey Mills, Bradley Wood, Crofton Hall(near Wakefield) or they took the Thornhill Midland-Royston line to the yards at Cudworth and Carlton or to Manvers Main, Wath.

Above: A mile and a half east of Mytholmroyd was Luddendenfoot station and its goods yard, seen here being passed at 9.3am on 7th August, 1961 by Stanier Black Five 4-6-0 No. 44692 heading the 7am Southport to Leeds Central and Bradford Exchange. (*Robert Anderson*)

Below: Heavy goods engines the big 9F 2-10-0s may have been, but they could put up a good show with an express passenger train when needed and they started appearing on summer Saturday extras through the Calder Valley in 1957. Here, Toton-based 92113 bowls an excursion from the East Midlands past the gardens at Luddendenfoot station on the same day as above. (*Robert Anderson*)

Luddendenfoot goods yard had a five ton crane and could handle most traffic except furniture vans, carriages, motor cars and machines on wheels. It became an unstaffed public delivery siding when the passenger station closed on 10th September, 1962, closing completely on 3rd May, 1965.

Above: Luddendenfoot station was in a fairly tight space as illustrated by this view of BR Class 4 4-6-0 No. 75048 speeding through with the 12.55 Leeds/1.15pm Bradford-Liverpool express on 7th August, 1961. Liverpool's Bank Hall shed had to use Class 4 power on these trains in 1961 owing to a shortage of the usual Class 5s. Little remains of the station in 1998. *(Robert Anderson)*

Below: The L&Y 0-6-0s were mainly goods engines but could still be seen hauling passenger stock. Aspinall 3F No.12289 of the LMS was passing Cooper House between Luddendenfoot and Sowerby Bridge in 1938. Sixty years later the area around this view is heavily overgrown with trees. *(Jack Wild collection)*

Right: Cooper House Sidings signal box, east of Luddendenfoot, controlled connections to Luddendenfoot gas works and Whitworth's works. The 20-lever box pictured in September, 1965 - the year it closed - is not the original which dated from 1874, but a second hand replacement installed in 1947. The box had no piped water and cans were delivered on the morning Sowerby Bridge-Hebden Bridge trip. *(Jack Wild / S. Chapman collection)*

Left: These big 4-6-0s designed by Hughes and introduced in 1920 were intended to be the L&Y's premier express locomotives.

Affectionately known as the "Dreadnaughts" they hauled some of the principal trains through the Calder Valley until the last of them was withdrawn from service in 1950.

In 1938, LMS No. 10412 heads empty stock east of Luddendenfoot. *(Jack Wild collection)*

Bottom: Another example of L&Y big engine power. Hughes 4-6-4 "Baltic" tank No. 11116 was on an eastbound stopper between Luddendenfoot and Sowerby Bridge during 1938. In those days even local passenger trains were of considerable length. They are usually just two-car diesel units nowadays. *(Jack Wild collection))*

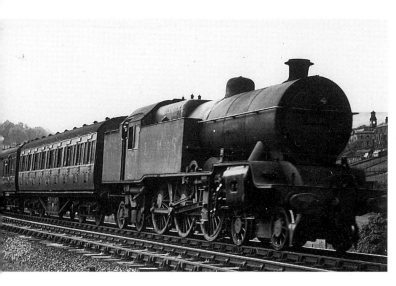

In 1957 the fastest Manchester-Leeds Calder Valley time was 95 minutes. Dieselisation in 1962 cut it to 86 minutes but in 1998 it was 91 minutes.

Above: With Wainhouse Tower reaching up from the horizon, LMS 2P 4-4-0 No. 676 steams a west-bound 1938 local over Luddendenfoot water troughs. *(Jack Wild collection)*

Below: Coming the other way, L&Y Aspinall/Hughes "Radial" 3P 2-4-2T LMS No.10945 collects water from Luddendenfoot troughs while heading east with a stopping train in 1938.
The Radial tanks were real maids of all work and until the 1950s could be seen on practically any sort of traffic. *(Locophotos)*

Right: Patriot 4-6-0 No. 45517 passing Sowerby Bridge loco depot and heading towards the tunnel with the combined 1.55pm Leeds/2.15pm Bradford-Liverpool on 7th August, 1961.

The Co-op flour mill complete with its own rail warehouse is above left, Sowerby Bridge West signal box(destroyed by fire in 1985) and the goods yard are on the right. *(Robert Anderson)*

SHORT MEMORIES

25.9.58: Crewe LNWR-design 0-8-0 49454 collects empty coaches from Dewsbury C&W works then hauls the 4pm Mirfield-Cleckheaton, 5.4 Cleckheaton-Clayton West and 6.35 Clayton West-Mirfield.

20.6.59: K3 2-6-0 61825 brings the Poole-Bradford into Halifax after B1 No. 61049 fails on the outward run.

Below: Down at ground level and looking towards Sowerby Bridge Tunnel. Visiting Hull K3 2-6-0 No. 61935 has joined "Crab" 2-6-0 No. 42715 alongside the coaling stage as Ivatt Class 2 2-6-0 No. 46438 goes off shed at 5.44pm on 7th August, 1961. *(Robert Anderson)*

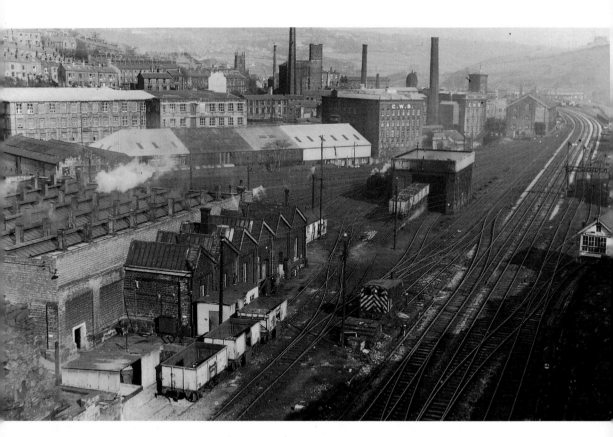

Above: A panoramic view of Sowerby Bridge motive power depot from above the tunnel on 27th March, 1963 showing the rebuilt shed, combined water tower and coaling stage, and a 204hp 0-6-0 diesel shunter sitting in its usual place. *(Jack Wild/Stephen Chapman collection)*

One of Sowerby Bridge motive power depot's main functions was to provide locomotives for freight and shunt workings at Mytholmroyd and Greetland yards but it also supplied engines for local passenger and parcels services. It even had the odd express turn on York trains.

Built in 1887 to replace a converted carriage shed, it was coded 25E in the LM Region's Wakefield district until 1957 when the district transferred to the North Eastern Region and it became 56E. In 1962 56E became the last refuge of the ex-L&Y 0-6-0s. The depot closed along with Mytholmroyd yard in January, 1964 and was demolished in 1965 though the coaling stage remains, redeveloped for other use. In 1998 the site is used by a road haulage firm distributing beer casks.

Locomotives allocated to Sowerby Bridge, Autumn, 1962

Fairburn Class 4 2-6-4T: 42094/151
Fowler Class 4 2-6-4T: 42405
Aspinall 3F 0-6-0:52121/413/61/515
WD 2-8-0: 90113/22/90200/10/33/81/
310/29/60/ 412/70/692

Total: 19

Left: Until the late 1950s the L&Y Aspinall 0-6-0STs were regular pilots around the whole area. LMS No. 11500 is pictured at Sowerby Bridge shed in the 1930s. *(Jack Wild collection)*

Right: A trio of redundant Fairburn 2-6-4Ts line up in the shed yard with L&Y 0-6-0s 52461 and 52413 in summer, 1962. No. 42150 went to Wakefield shed where it remained until being withdrawn in late 1966. *(Peter Cookson)* In the mid-1950s, Sowerby Bridge 2-6-4Ts worked the 10-coach 5.15pm York-Manchester express from Wakefield and on Saturdays they piloted the 9.30am Manchester-Glasgow as far as Bolton.

Left: Ex-L&Y 3F 0-6-0 No. 52408 bearing a 25E shedplate stands inside the shed during reroofing in the early 1950s. Outside is a 2-6-4T and one of the two ex-LMS 0-6-0Ts then allocated there.

Below: Movements to and from Sowerby Bridge shed were normally controlled by the quaint River Bridge ground frame box, still there in August, 1967. *(Both Jack Wild / Stephen Chapman collection)*

A telephone is provided on a post between the shed coal ramp road and No. 1 ashpit road at the exit from Sowerby Bridge engine shed to enable trainmen to communicate with the person in charge at River Bridge ground frame or the signalman at Station box when the ground frame is closed... The telephone must be used in all cases of engines leaving the shed whether the shed outlet signal (No.6) worked from the ground frame is clear or not. *B.R. N.E. Region Sectional Appendix, 1960.*

Above: It is February, 1964, Sowerby Bridge shed is closed and awaiting demolition. With no locos present, a clear view of the facilities can be had. (*Jack Wild / Stephen Chapman collection*)

On the day these photos were taken the arrangements board on the shed wall showed the last day's loco position. In the Special workings column were five light engines - No. 52515 to Didcot, another two including 92221 to Reading, and 42150 to Southall. At the top of the engine column for freight workings was A4 Pacific No. 60001 light engine, and engines booked for trains from Mytholmroyd to Carlisle, Aintree, Bury, Blackpool, Glasgow and Penzance. Locos shown as receiving attention from the fitters were 77014 and 78011; 15 locos were shown as "stabled in the yard" on 10 roads along with the message "Go by bus." Most bizarre of all was the list of locos at main works which included 46123, 45555, 49160, 45501, 45508 and 90736. It all looks like somebody's idea of a "last day" joke although in late 1963 East Coast Pacifics did reach the Calder Valley on freights from the North East to Healey Mills and could the "main works" list have been locos passing through on their way to a scrapyard? Not 90736 though - there was no such engine.

Below: Looking east with the goods depots on the right, including the Halifax Farmers' shed right of the coal stage and the Co-op flour mill left.(*Jack Wild / Stephen Chapman collection*)

Above: Showing that the Calder Valley saw steam to the bitter end, 8F 2-8-0 No. 48702 heads an express freight past the goods depot on 27th April, 1968. *(Jack Wild / Stephen Chapman collection)*

Below: In 1980 there was still enough freight traffic at Halifax, including ferry vans for the Continent, to warrant its own pilot loco outstationed from Bradford. A regular was BR/Gardner 204hp 0-6-0 shunter No. 03371 and its duties included tripping coal wagons to the still open coal depot at Sowerby Bridge. Known to Halifax staff as *"Mavis"*, 03371 is seen in Sowerby Bridge yard. *Mavis* had to be coupled with a match truck as her wheelbase was too short to operate track circuits reliably. Sowerby Bridge coal traffic ended in the early 1980s. *(Malcolm Roughley)*

In 1956 Sowerby Bridge had a 10 ton capacity yard crane and could handle all kinds of goods, parcels, livestock and mineral traffic. Private sidings served the Co-op Wholesale Society's flour mill and the Hollings Mill Estate Co. General freight mostly disappeared in the 1960s but coal was still received.

Above: Having arrived with a portion of Blackpool excursion 1X11, BR Standard Class 3 2-6-0 No. 77012, from Farnley Junction shed, Leeds, waits patiently at the west end of Sowerby Bridge station while Black Five No. 45104 passes with an eastbound parcels train on 26th September, 1964.

Below: Spectacular for the photographer but not a good advert for steam. This was utterly filthy 8F 2-8-0 No. 48547 blasting a Healey Mills to Bolton freight through Sowerby Bridge station on a decidedly leaden 19th March, 1964. Until the late 1960s, this station had six platform faces but they were subsequently reduced to just the two main line platforms and the whole place became totally unstaffed in August, 1985. *(Both Jack Wild / Stephen Chapman collection)*

Above: The Northern Rubber Company's annual Blackpool outing was notable for bringing an East Coast Pacific to the Calder Valley. The October, 1963 trip brought A1 No. 601 14 *W. P. Allen* which stopped for water at Sowerby Bridge. The station buildings are on the right.

"My lasting memory of travelling on the Leeds/Bradford-Liverpool expresses is the other passengers in their mohair suits with large suitcases carrying Cunard labels," *Robert Anderson.*

Below: Jubilee 45694 *Bellerophon* awaits departure with Bradford-Blackpool special 1X11 on 26th September, 1964. The wagons mark the now preserved coal drops. *(Jack Wild / S. Chapman collection)*

Above: The magnificent Tudor-style station buildings at Sowerby Bridge, sadly now long gone after being destroyed by fire in the 1970s. When this picture was taken in January, 1964 they contained station master's offices as well as various passenger and parcels facilities. All that remained in 1998 was the single storey building to the right of the A1 on page 43.
(Jack Wild / Stephen Chapman collection)

Bernard Whitaker was station master at Sowerby Bridge from 1965 to 1970.

"The main buildings were partly modernised but many original features survived. My office still boasted an L&Y sloping mahogany counter and an old wooden rack in the parcels office held scores of L&YR luggage labels to such places as Blackburn, Padiham and Blackpool Talbot Road.

"The station was a hive of activity with a full staff comprising two foremen, four porters, a lampman, 14 signalmen, three clerks for the parcels and booking offices, two shunters for the yard and a van driver for parcels deliveries.

"Some of the staff took great pride in their workplace and we had a long-established lawned garden and fishpond stocked with golden carp. These drew appreciative comments from passengers and Sowerby Bridge never failed to win a top prize in the annual regional station gardens competition. This was due largely to the efforts of chief clerk Len Hopkinson, who looked after the garden, and porter Billy Clare who attended the fish.

"In 1965 the powers-that-be decided to demolish the loco shed using explosives. An 'expert' assured us that it was the safest and most effective way of clearing the site but when the dust cleared all the pillars which were supposed to be reduced to rubble were still standing but most of the windows had been blown out of the Co-op bakery.

"Another incident involved a rogue bogie bolster wagon in a freight train bound for Healey Mills. The signalman at Station box alerted me after hearing a lot of noise from the train. Checking the track just east of the station I found evidence of derailment damage and sent a message via Control to have the train put in the loop at Mirfield for examination. It transpired that the wagon had derailed on the Down Bay outlet points at Sowerby Bridge station and had been dragged with one bogie off the rails to Milner Royd Junction where it rerailed itself.

"Summer Saturdays and Bank Holidays were very busy and I made a point of being available to attend to trains. Most were still steam in 1965 and the station's old water tower saw regular use.

"One of the most spectacular regular steam workings in the mid-1960s was the Newcastle to Manchester Red Bank van train which was always heavily loaded and double-headed. It used to hammer through the station at high speed.

"Steam dwindled markedly during the latter part of 1967 as more diesels became available, notably class 37s and 40s from Healey Mills, and by spring 1968 was restricted to a few Lancashire freights.

"My sphere of responsibility was extended to Mytholmroyd and Hebden Bridge in 1969 by which time steam had gone and excursion traffic had all but ceased."

Above: Behind Sowerby Bridge station was the start of the branch to Rishworth. This picture is not what it seems, though. Passenger services had long since been withdrawn and Ivatt Class 4 2-6-0 No. 43116 was simply shunting an ex-works suburban coach on one of the branch roads near the site of the Sowerby Bridge station halt at 6.38pm on 7th August, 1961. *(Robert Anderson)*

Below: One of the L&Y steam railmotors introduced on the Rishworth branch in 1907 to compete with electric trams calls at Triangle station, known locally as "Happy Jack's" *(Jack Wild collection)*

In 1910 Rishworth had a remarkably good weekday service with a railmotor making 18 return trips.

Trains left Watson Crossing halt, Sowerby Bridge at 7.1, 7.38, 8.21, 9, 10.11, 10.42, 11.15 am, 12.6, 1.1, 2.1, 2.48, 4.18, 5.11, 6.12, 7.21, 8.26, 9.1, 9.43 and 10.51pm SO. Turnround times at Rishworth varied from two to 16 minutes. Journey times were 13 minutes outward and 11 return.

Left: The tram-stop type facilities at Watson Crossing Halt near Sowerby Bridge around 1910. *(Jack Wild collection)*

In 1956 Ripponden could handle general goods, minerals, horse boxes and cattle vans. Like Stainland and West Vale, it had a 1.5 ton yard crane.

Below: 1/2500 map of Rishworth in 1930. *(By courtesy of the Ordnance Survey)*

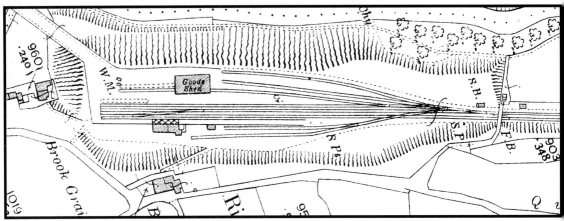

Below: Looking east from Sowerby Bridge station in October, 1958 towards the junction with the Ripponden branch which goes off to the right. The main line passes behind the station signal box on the left and an ex-L&Y 0-6-0 simmers in the sunshine.

SHORT MEMORIES

22.7.59: BR Clan Pacific 72000 *Clan Buchanan* of Glasgow Polmadie is on the 7.47am Todmorden-Manchester Victoria.

May, 1960: Royal Scot 46102 *Black Watch* and Clan Pacific 72001 *Clan Cameron* of Glasgow Polmadie, and 46106 *Gordon Highlander* of Manchester Longsight, all have turns on the 7.47 Todmorden-Manchester.

30.7.60: K3s 61856 and 61932 double head a Blackpool-Sheffield relief through Calderdale. Crosti-boilered 9F 92025 heads a Mytholmroyd-Ramsbottom freight.

Summer, 1960: Ardsley K3s power the 8.25am Bradford-Blackpool and 7.33pm return.

17.9.60: Camden based Royal Scot 46144 *Honourable Artillery Company* is on the 6.47pm Manchester Vic.-Todmorden.

Above: Viewed from Sowerby Bridge Station box, Black Five No. 45104 from Bolton shed heads an eastbound train of loose-coupled empties on 27th April, 1968.

Below: When the North Eastern authorities took over the Calder Valley east of Eastwood, ex-LNER locomotives became more commonplace. J39 0-6-0 No. 64791, seen backing east through the station in August, 1962, was one of a batch then stationed at Low Moor. Sowerby Bridge Station signal box on the right was abolished on 4th March, 1973.
(Both Jack Wild / Stephen Chapman collection)

Above: Another Black Five - but what we would give for a sight like this on today's bland and boring railway. An unidentifiable member of the class pulls out of Sowerby Bridge with a Manchester- Filey Holiday Camp excursion in July, 1965. *(Jack Wild / Stephen Chapman collection)*

On Easter Monday, 19th April, 1965, the station master's son, Alan Whitaker, observed these excursions at Sowerby Bridge:

Time	Train	Loco
08.54 pass 1X36	Leeds-Blackpool	45643 *Rodney*
09.02 stop 1X30	Heckmondwike-Morecambe	61123
09.10 pass 1X37	Bradford Ex.-Blackpool	44694
09.28 stop 1X08	Bradford Ex.-Southport	61386
09.32 stop 1X39	Castleford-Blackpool	61022 *Sassaby*
	Stopped for water	
09.59 pass 1X06	Chesterfield-Blackpool	D5848
10.07 pass 1X46	Cleckheaton-Blackpool	44946
10.13 stop 1X47	Low Moor-Blackpool	61189 *Sir William Gray*
10.23 loop 1X12	Bradford Ex.-Belle Vue	61240 *Harry Hinchcliffe*
10.29 pass 1X44	Bradford Ex.-Blackpool	44695
11.21 stop 1X18	Lightcliffe-Belle Vue	61259

On Easter Monday, 1966 the Cleckheaton, Low Moor and Lightcliffe trains had disappeared and Jubilees *Alberta, Victoria, Bellerophon, Ulster* and *Sturdee* hauled five of the eight trains. Black Fives 44990, 45208 and diesel D1772 worked the others.

On Saturday 12.6.65, he noted Britannia Pacific 70026 *Polar Star*, Jubilees 45581 *Bihar and Orissa*, 45643 *Rodney* and 45694 *Bellerophon*, B1 No. 61189 *Sir William Gray* and diesels D1801 and D5680 on Blackpool-bound excursions.

In summer, 1961 10 Down and 11 Up booked summer Saturday trains included the 9.35am Sowerby Bridge-Bridlington via Halifax and Cleckheaton, 8.50am Manchester Victoria-Scarborough Central, 9.5am Liverpool Ex.-Scarborough Londesborough Rd., 1.30pm Blackpool Central-Halifax Cleckheaton-Wakefield, 1.3? Blackpool Central-Barnsley 8.30am Heckmondwike Blackpool Central, 8.1? Hull-Blackpool Cen., 8.3? Barnsley-Blackpool Central 11.20am Scarborough Cen. Manchester Vic., 11.15am Scarborough Londesborough Rd.-Liverpool Exchange, as well as Bradford Leeds/York-Blackpool and Llandudno trains

Relief of trainmen working special passenger trains not booked to stop at Sowerby Bridge station must be effected as follows: Up line - Sowerby Bridge West signal box, Down line - No.1 Home Signal, Station box, at Manchester end of station platform. *B.R. N.E. Region Sectional Appendix, 1960.*

Above: On 29th September, 1962 the Halifax Railfans ran this memorable South Yorkshireman rail-tour to Darlington, hauled by Sowerby Bridge's own ex-L&Y 0-6-0 No. 52515 and ex-LMS 4F 0-6-0 No. 44408 from Normanton shed. They are seen awaiting the start of their journey. *(N.E. Stead collection)*

Below: Reputed to be the last steam-hauled train to Liverpool via the Calder Valley, this railtour on 27th April, 1968 approaches Sowerby Bridge from the east. It is double-headed by a pair of BR Standard Class 5 4-6-0s led by Caprotti valve gear-fitted No. 73134 of Manchester Patricroft shed. *(Jack Wild / Stephen Chapman collection)*

Above: Just under a mile east of Sowerby Bridge is Milner Royd Junction where the West Riding Union line up to Halifax curves off to the left. On this particular occasion in June, 1966, York English Electric Type 4 diesel No. D252 and a Black Five were approaching from the Wakefield direction with the Newcastle to Red Bank empty vans. *(Jack Wild / Stephen Chapman collection)*

Below: Jubilee 4-6-0 No. 45571 *South Afrca* heads east from Milner Royd and passes Copley Mills with an excursion bound for Filey on 20th July, 1963. The Halifax line over which all passenger trains now run climbs up to the right. *(Jack Wild / Stephen Chapman collection)*

Greetland, as it used to be.

Top: One mile 509 yards east of Milner Royd was the unpretty Greetland No. 1 signal box which controlled the western entrance to the sidings. This box was closed on 21st August, 1966.

Centre: Greetland Ground Frame box, looking east in June, 1964, controlled movements within the sidings which were situated between No. 1 box and the station.

Bottom: Greetland looking east, with houses, water tank and goods depot still intact in June, 1964. The station buildings, in the right distance, were just being demolished. *(All Jack Wild / Stephen Chapman collection)*

In 1956 Greetland goods yard was equipped to handle general goods, horse boxes and prize cattle vans. It had a 5 ton yard crane but mobile cranes were used when needed. The depot closed on 28th June, 1965 and the site became a rail-served oil distribution terminal.

Above: Manchester Newton Heath WD 2-8-0 No. 90376 rolls past Greetland yard, over the junction with the M&L Halifax branch and towards the station with an eastbound train of empty bogie bolster wagons on 30th September, 1961. *(P. B.Booth / N.E.Stead collection)*

Below: Right until the Greetland-Halifax line was mothballed in 1988, heavy trains needed banking up the 1 in 45 to Dryclough Junction. Here, Low Moor WD No. 90200 shoves the 6.15am Hillhouse to Laisterdyke Class 6 goods over the viaduct crossing the River Calder at the start of the climb on 3rd November, 1962. Another WD was on the front. *(Robert Anderson)*

Above: Beautifully turned out Black Five 4-6-0 No. 44694 finds the going easier as it comes down grade towards Greetland with the very last run of the 8.42am Halifax to St. Pancras through coaches on 3rd November, 1962. *(Robert Anderson)*

Left: Before completion of the West Riding Union this was the end of the line from Greetland. The first Halifax station at Shaw Syke in February, 1964. *(Jack Wild / Stephen Chapman collection.)*

Right: This view of another WD tanker at Salterhebble shows just how steep the Greetland-Dryclough line is. Trains sometimes took a run at the bank from Elland. *(Jack Wild collection).*

53

Above: Despite imminent closure on 10th September, 1962, Greetland station was still well kept and looking smart with its unusually attractive buildings on the left. Originally known as North Dean, Halifax passengers had to change here for a horse bus until the branch to Shaw Syke was opened in 1844. The station was renamed Greetland and North Dean in 1883 and Greetland in 1897. The unpicturesque Greetland No. 2 signal box, a standard wartime structure built by the LMS in 1941 to replace the original dating from 1878, remains in 1998 but is switched out of use. *(Jack Wild / Stephen Chapman collection)*

Below: By August, 1966 the scene at Greetland had changed considerably. The station and goods yard had been cleared and a new oil terminal built on the site. This view shows the first tanks to arrive on opening day. *(Jack Wild / Stephen Chapman collection)*

SHORT MEMORIES

1.10.60: Stanier 2-6-0 No. 42971 from Mold Junction, North Wales, is the Elland pilot.

October, 1960: The new 6.30am York Dringhouses-Liverpool Edge Hill express goods is the first Class 'C' fitted freight on the Calder Valley, normally a York or Mirfield B1.

18.10.60: Rebuilt Patriot 4-6-0 No. 45526 *Morecambe and Heysham* of Carlisle Upperby shed leaves Todmorden with the 7.51am to Manchester Victoria.

April, 1961: Four of Newton Heath's Britannia Pacifics have turns on the 7.51am Todmorden-Manchester.

Above: Ex-LMS Hughes/Fowler "Crab" Class 5 2-6-0 No. 42849 enters Greetland station from the east with a local train of large coal on 30th September, 1961. The proud owner of the racer bike on the left would have been the envy of his pals at the time. (*P. B. Booth / N. E. Stead collection*)

Below: Unusual power for the Newcastle-Red Bank empty newspaper vans on 28th May, 1963 was 9F 2-10-0 No. 92126 which has just emerged from the hill separating Greetland from Elland. The remains of the branch to Stainland cut across the foreground. (*David Holmes*)

Top: Although just 1.75 miles long, the Stainland branch was built to fairly substantial proportions. West Vale, viewed towards Greetland and hosting an L&Y railmotor, looked more like a main line station. *(Jack Wild collection)*

Back in 1910 Stainland enjoyed a service of 17 railmotors each way on weekdays. Most trains ran to and from Halifax, taking 13 minutes each way. They ran as late as 10.35pm from Halifax and 10.50pm from Stainland.

Bottom: Aspinall 3F 0-6-0 No. 52411 wanders about the weeds at Stainland and Holywell Green in July, 1958. By this time Stainland goods yard, to the right, only handled coal, mostly for Brookroyd mill, and would close in two months' time.

Centre: No. 52411 near West Vale while on its way back to Greetland. *(Both Hugh Davies)*

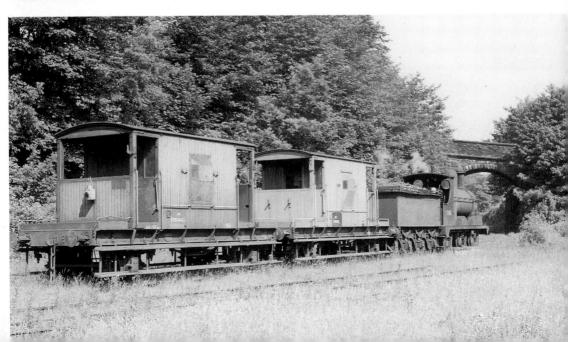

SHORT MEMORIES

8.4.61: Willesden-based Britannia No. 70032 *Tennyson* is on the 5.35pm Manchester Victoria-Todmorden.

6.5.61: A3 Pacific 60103 *Flying Scotsman* hauls the return leg of a Gainsborough Model Railway Society Lincoln-Keswick railtour via Copy Pit and Mirfield.

Sept. 1962: Over-crowding at peak times is now a problem on the DMUs which replaced steam last January; they also have insufficient room for parcels.

Sept. 1962: Three L&Y 0-6-0s at Sowerby Bridge are the last active members of their class.

19.9.62: Edge Hill Royal Scot No. 46124 *London Scottish* heads a York-Oldham special freight along the Calder Valley.

Above: Huddersfield-based Fowler Class 4 2-6-4T No. 42408 brings the Saturday only 10am Bradford-Poole out of Elland Tunnel and towards the station at 10.22 on 27th July, 1963. *(David Holmes)*

Elland goods facilities in 1956 included a covered two-face dock with an end-loading dock included, an 8 ton yard crane and a large wool and grain warehouse. The depot could handle all kinds of goods, including coal, minerals, furniture vans, motor cars, carriages, portable engines, machines on wheels, livestock, horse boxes and prize cattle vans, and carriages and motor cars by passenger or parcels train. A private siding near Elland served the works of Wm. Hawkyard & Son as well as the Band Clays Co.

Below: Elland station viewed from the goods dock at 5.16pm on 26th April, 1963 with Black Five 4-6-0 No. 44895 and "Crab" 2-6-0 No. 42943 heading the 9.31am Newcastle-Red Bank vans.
(David Holmes)

Elland station on 30th September, 1962, 20 days after closure but still retaining plenty of L&Y character.

Top: Looking east.

Centre: Looking west.

Bottom: The sign says it all about the destinations once served by trains from the westbound platform.
(All Jack Wild / Stephen Chapman collection)

In 1957 Elland was served by trains to Normanton, Halifax, Bradford, Sowerby Bridge, Manchester, Blackpool, Huddersfield, Penistone, Stockport, Holmfirth and Clayton West. Hopefully, there will be a station at Elland again by the year 2000 when a new Halifax-Huddersfield service starts running.

SHORT MEMORIES

22.8.63: A3 No. 60045 *Lemberg* arrives at Mirfield with a freight from Tyne Yard. A4 No. 60006 *Sir Ralph Wedgewood* does the same on 13th Sept.

Easter 1965: Most excursions to the Lancashire coast are worked by B1 or Black Five 4-6-0s, but there are only half as many as in previous years.

April, 1966: About 30 steam-hauled freights a day still pass through Brighouse.

For just over a year from March, 1963, David Holmes was station master at Elland with responsibility for Greetland as well.

He recalls that Elland was "a dreary place of dark, satanic mills."

Greetland and Elland stations were closed but each had a coal yard while fire bricks for steam locos were forwarded from Elland to sheds all over the country in specially adapted wagons.

"On average there were about 90 trains through Elland every 24 hours. They included the Normanton-Halifax parcels, often just one 4-wheel van with Fowler 2-6-4T 42406 a regular loco. We had B16 4-6-0s on several Mirfield-Mytholmroyd trips a day. The Halifax-King's Cross came through each morning, usually worked by Fairburn tank 42116, and at 4pm the Halifax-Stockport passenger with its Palethorpes Sausages van at the rear. A Carlisle-Halifax freight sometimes produced a Royal Scot: 46142 on 17th June, 1963, 46150 on 23rd October and 46157 on 28th November. No. 46115 worked an Up coal train on 7th March; 4F 44056 with self weighing tender was sometimes on the 9.15am Brighouse-Greetland trip. Jubilees were regulars on summer Saturday trains, 45620 with the 7.15am Long Eaton-Blackpool on 27th July, and 45565 with the 8.15am Filey Holiday Camp-Preston.

"A 4F 0-6-0, often 43968, stood by Greetland No.2 signal box ready to bank the occasional train up to Dryclough. It also shunted Elland and Greetland

"Once, a heavy concrete sleeper train passed Elland en-route to Halifax with two WDs at the front. One was to come off at Greetland and bank the train but the train stormed through without stopping - the guard signalling frantically to the signalman, having removed the tail lamp from his van to emphasise the point. The train got up the bank without any wagons breaking away but it could have turned into an unfortunate incident.

"Around the same time a 3-car York-Manchester DMU caught fire. Greetland No.2 signalman sent seven bells on the block bell to Greetland No.1. I commandeered a passing 4F to go to the scene. When I arrived, the fire brigade was there but the guard had put the fire out using the train extinguishers. We propelled the unit to Sowerby Bridge where the passengers changed to another train.

"The power station was the reason for keeping a station master at Elland; its coal came in four loose-coupled trains a day, all from the Brighouse end, entering the power station by a facing main to main crossover.

"During the power station's construction a huge transformer came from Tyneside by road and then had to be shipped to a special rail wagon for the last half mile as a road bridge was too narrow."

In Spring, 1964 the Elland SM's job was divided between Brighouse and Sowerby Bridge, David Holmes becoming a temporary summer relief SM.

Looking east from above the tunnel towards Elland station in August, 1964 after the buildings had been demolished. The modern signal box, which replaced Waterhouse Siding, Elland East and West boxes in May, 1958 and is still used in 1998, is to the right of the far end of the platform. The goods yard closed on 28th June,1962 and the large warehouse, latterly used by a firm making furniture from old railway sleepers, was demolished early in 1998. (*Jack Wild / S. Chapman collection*)

On 18th December, 1963, David Holmes logged these steam movements at Elland: 9.18am the 9.12 Halifax-Kings Cross on the Down Main hauled by 2-6-4T 42116; **9.36** the 7.30 Wakefield-Rose Grove on the Up Main behind WD 2-8-0 90555; **9.42** 8F 2-8-0 48162 on the 4.18am Aintree-Crofton while WD 90200 was the pilot in the Up Loop; **10.4** Black Five 44887 on the Up Main with the 2.23am Carlisle-Halifax express freight; **10.33** 8F 48070 took the 2.50am Manchester Brewery Sidings-Healey Mills via the Down Loop; **11.6** a Neville Hill-Rose Grove freight hauled by 8F 48067on the Up Main; **11.16** 2-6-4T 42622 on the Down Main going light to Huddersfield Hillhouse; **11.18** WD 90665 takes the Up No.1 line with the 8am Normanton-Todmorden goods; **11.22** the 9am Carlton-Mytholmroyd hauled by 90171 on the Up Main; **11.28** WD 90707 on the Down Main with the 5.40am Bamber Bridge-Healey Mills; **11.47** 90413 on the Up Main going light to Sowerby Bridge; **12.4pm** 8F 48294 on the Up Main with the 9.55am Bolton Haliwell Street-Sharlston; **12.8** B1 61131 on the Up Main with the 11.55 Healey Mills-Mytholmroyd; **12.10** the 9.52 Radcliffe-Healey Mills on the Down Main with 8F 48164; and at **12.17** Black Five 44782 on the Up Main with the 9.38 York-Manchester parcels.

For internal shunting at Elland power station the Central Electricity Generating Board had a Hudswell Clarke diesel mechanical 0-4-0 built in 1959, *Elland No.1,* and a John Fowler diesel hydraulic 0-4-0 built in 1960, *Elland No. 2.*
Here the Fowler moves 16-ton coal wagons on the shunting neck alongside the main line in 1976.
(Stephen Chapman)

Before a train departs from either of the Reception lines at Elland power station....the guard must first obtain the authority of the signalman by the telephone positioned between the hand points giving access to the Reception lines and those giving access to the Exchange sidings....Should a second train need to be admitted to the CEGB sidings before the first is ready to depart, the Elland signalman must obtain an assurance by telephone from the guard of the first train that his train is clear of all points, the Single line and one Reception line is clear....*BR N.E. Region Sectional Appendix, 1960.*

In late 1962 Elland power station was fed by two morning coal trains from Wath, Tues - Sat with an extra on Saturday evenings and one early on Sunday mornings, all worked by Brush Type 2 diesels, plus two daytime arrivals, Mon-Sat, from Penistone Barnsley Junction hauled by Wakefield WDs.

Below: With its headboard, crimson and cream coaches and smartly turned out Black Five No. 44912, the Bradford to Marylebone South Yorkshireman makes a real sight for sore eyes while passing Waterhouse Sidings, Elland, on 18th June, 1955. *(Arthur Wilson)*

Above: WD 2-8-0 No. 90639 rumbles through Brighouse station with a long eastbound train of empty coal wagons. Most returning empties ran as class 7 loose-coupled express freights not fitted with continuous brakes, as denoted by 90639's headlamps. Brighouse station closed to passengers when the York-Manchester Victoria direct service was withdrawn on 5th January, 1970, making it the biggest town in West Yorkshire without a rail passenger service. The overgrown platforms remain in 1998 and hopefully the station will be open again by the year 2000, served by a revived Halifax-Huddersfield service. Goods facilities, already reduced to a public delivery siding, were withdrawn on 7th September, 1970. *(N. E. Stead collection)*

Below: Coming the other way with Brighouse Exchange sidings behind them, Jubilee No. 45700 *Britannia* and a Black Five double head the Newcastle- Red Bank vans off the four track section and on to the double track main line. *(Tony Ross)*

Right: Anchor Pit Junction, where the line to Bailiff Bridge and Wyke Junction left the Calder Valley main line and went off to the right.

This view was taken on 30th July, 1967, the day the box closed, by which time the junction provided only access to Brighouse sidings.
(Jack Wild / Stephen Chapman collection)

BRIGHOUSE - RELIEVING OF TRAINMEN: Telephones are provided in the lamp room on the Up platform, and in the porters' room on the Down platform, to enable trainmen to communicate with the Control office at Wakefield. The following arrangements must be carried out by all concerned:

Down line-Trains stopping at Brighouse for traffic purposes to be relieved at Exchange Sidings.

Trains not stopping at Brighouse but stopping at Bradley Wood for traffic purposes to be relieved at Bradley Wood.

Trains not stopping at Brighouse or Bradley Wood for traffic purposes to be relieved at Brighouse station.

Up line-All trains to be relieved at Brighouse Station box.

DOWN ARRIVAL LINE: Drivers in charge of movements from Anchor Pit to the Exchange sidings over the Down Arrival line, must not foul the scissors crossing points until they receive instructions to do so from the ground staff. *BR N.E. Region Sectional Appendix, 1960.*

Left: Between Bradley Wood and Heaton Lodge junctions was Cooper Bridge, originally the Manchester & Leeds station for Huddersfield.

Despite the opening of railways into Huddersfield itself within a few years, Cooper Bridge station survived until February, 1950. Its small goods depot, unstaffed since 1958, closed in 1963.
(Lens of Sutton)

Above: Jubilee 4-6-0 No. 45719 *Glorious* speeds over the River Calder with the 10.30am Liverpool Exchange to Newcastle express in 1954. *Glorious,* one of three Jubilees kept by Liverpool Bank Hall shed for this duty, is crossing the original M&L stone bridge, the girder bridge being added during the 1890s widening. Beyond the bridge are the remains of Cooper Bridge station. *(Tony Ross)*

Right: No. 45716 *Swiftsure* on less glorious work, heading an eastbound unfitted express freight over Heaton Lodge Junction. The line to Huddersfield curves left. *(J. Wild / S. Chapman collection)*

Below: Even on a summer Saturday with all the demands on motive power and line capacity, mineral traffic still had to be moved. 8F No. 48506 from Liverpool Speke Junction brings eastbound empties off the Huddersfield line as Black Five No.44781 approaches with a seaside excursion on 19th August, 1961. *(Peter Rose)*

Above: Viewed from the old formation of the Midland line to Huddersfield, an unsung WD 2-8-0 trundles an eastbound train of empties past a forest of semaphores protecting Heaton Lodge Junction. The back of the train is passing Heaton Lodge signal box while the LNW "New Line" to Leeds is on the extreme right having just passed under the L&Y main line. The whole area was remodelled in 1970 but, apart from the removal of the semaphores, the box and some track, the scene looks remarkably similar in 1998, the "New Line" being connected to the L&Y Down side since the remodelling.

Below: A little further towards Mirfield, with the bulk of Battyeford girder bridge carrying the "New Line" over the River Calder dominating the background, Newton Heath 8F 2-8-0 No. 48557 ambles along at the head of an eastbound class 7 freight in June, 1966.
(Jack Wild / Stephen Chapman collection)

Above: The Stanlow-Leeds oil tanks with 8F No. 48267 piloting a 9F 2-10-0 run neck and neck with Black Five No. 45353 on an eastbound express freight between Heaton Lodge and Mirfield. Compare this scene with today's lines of lorries on the M62. *(Jack Wild/Stephen Chapman collection)*

The speed signalling system was installed at Mirfield in 1932 with the aim of indicating to drivers the speed they should observe rather than the direction of the route set.

Searchlight signals were used in which one lamp could display a red, yellow or green aspect. The system was complicated, to say the least, and must have been a nightmare for drivers to learn. On plain line two reds meant stop, one yellow meant caution, prepare to stop at next signal, two yellows meant pass next signal at restricted speed, and single green meant clear. On junction signals, the top light referred to the main line(high speed) and the centre light to the diverging "medium speed" line. Main line aspects could be three reds meaning stop, yellow over red over red meaning caution, prepare to stop at next signal, two yellows over two reds meaning pass next signal at restricted speed, and green over two reds meaning clear, proceed. For the diverging routes, the aspects could be three reds meaning stop, red over yellow over red meaning caution, prepare to stop at next signal, red over two yellows over red meaning pass next signal at restricted speed, and red over green over red meaning clear. The bottom red was a marker light designed to draw attention to the system and was not lit when plain line green or yellow aspects were shown, but it could show yellow when used as a calling-on signal. Signals controlling low speed movements to loops or sidings showed two reds for stop, one red and a small green for proceed at low speed, or three reds for stop and two reds over small green for proceed at low speed. There were other combinations, such as yellow over green over red over red marker on a junction signal which meant pass second signal on high speed route at restricted speed. In addition, bracket signals indicating the direction of travel were provided for Heaton Lodge and Thornhill LNW junctions.

Below: Fairburn 2-6-4T No. 42084 of Low Moor enters the section of line controlled by the American-style speed signalling with a Halifax-London express portion on 10th August, 1961. Some Heaton Lodge bracket signals are in the right distance. *(Peter Cookson)*

Above: Mirfield engine shed in May, 1966 with 8F 2-8-0 No. 48026 simmering outside.
(Jack Wild / Stephen Chapman collection)

Supplying mainly freight locomotives, Mirfield shed was coded 25D in the LMS and BR London
Midland Region Wakefield district until 1957 when the district was transferred to the North
Eastern Region and it became 56D. While Sowerby Bridge retained its L&Y/LMS character to the
end, Mirfield's locomotive allocation began to come under strong NE influence soon after the
switch, not least the B16 4-6-0s exiled from their native territory around York, Leeds, Hull and
Scarborough.

The new Healey Mills diesel depot opened in 1966 soon rendered Mirfield shed redundant. It
closed to steam on 2nd January, 1967 when its last few steam locos were sent to Wakefield but it
remained a diesel stabling point until April. The shed survives in 1998 - as a road tanker depot.

LOCOMOTIVES ALLOCATED TO MIRFIELD JUNE, 1961

Fairburn Class 4 2-6-4T: 42152/285; Fowler Class 4 2-6-4T: 42406/7; 4F 0-6-0: 44056/474; 8F 2-8-
0: 48055/76/138/202/65/76/357/8/608; 3F 0-6-0: 52121/515; B1 4-6-0: 61040 *Roedeer*/1161/1230
B16/1 4-6-0: 61411/2/3/4/47; WD 2-8-0: 90184/300/457/622/98/721/3/31. Total 33

LOCOMOTIVES ON MIRFIELD SHED AT 3PM SATURDAY 15.4.61

Fairburn 2-6-4T: 42152/285; Fowler 2-6-4T: 42406; Stanier 6P5F 2-6-0: 42948; 4F 0-6-0: 44056
"Black Five" 4-6-0: 45248/5412; 8F 2-8-0: 48055/76/276/357/8/684; 3F 0-6-0: 52121/515; B16/1 4-6-0:
61411/3/4/6/47; WD 2-8-0: 90271/300/66/604/622/721/31. Total: 27

On Mirfield turntable in 1963, WD 2-8-0 90402, visiting from Lees, Oldham.
(Jack Wild / S. Chapman collection)

Above: Fairburn 2-6-4T No. 42150 passes Mirfield engine shed on 15th April, 1961 while working the 12 o'clock Bolton to Normanton stopping train. (*David Holmes*)

Left: For a time, the ex-L&Y shed at Mirfield had a stud of exiled ex-North Eastern Railway B16 4-6-0s which were used for transfer freights between Healey Mills, Mirfield and Mytholmroyd yards. B16/1 No. 61447 stands alongside the shed on 10th August, 1961. (*Peter Cookson*)

Right: In LMS days, the driver of Fowler 2-6-4T 2405 oils round before going off Mirfield shed to work a train. An ex-L&Y 2-4-2T stands alongside. (*W. Hubert Foster / courtesy John Holroyd*)

Fastest Man. Vic.-York time in 1998 was 2hr 13 minutes via Bradford compared with 2hr 6mins direct with steam and 1hr 51 minutes by direct DMU.

Above: Double-heading on the 2.15pm Saturdays Only Wakefield Kirkgate to Manchester Victoria express was just one of the spectacles to be enjoyed on the Calder Valley line in steam days. Here, B1 4-6-0s 61069 and 61024 *Addax* do the honours while racing past the Mirfield shed coaling stage at 2.29pm on 15th April, 1961. (*David Holmes*)

Below: Another stirring spectacle at the same spot. WD 2-8-0 No. 90604 on a westbound class 8 Through Freight overtakes a Black Five on similar duty while 8F 2-8-0 No. 48522 is in the shed yard. *(Peter Cookson)*

Above: Nowadays parcels and mail traffic like this is hard to find on station platforms but on 23rd March, 1961 this short parcels train with Huddersfield-based Fowler 2-6-4T No. 42410 was picking up a good load at Mirfield station. *(Peter Rose)*

Below: With the black, pitch-coated trainshed roof of Mirfield station looming above, Jubilee No. 45593 *Kholapur* lets off steam while awaiting departure with an eastbound special in 1966. Dating from 1866, this station was once an important interchange between the L&Y and LNWR. Facilities for passengers even included a billiard room. *(Jack Wild / Stephen Chapman collection)*

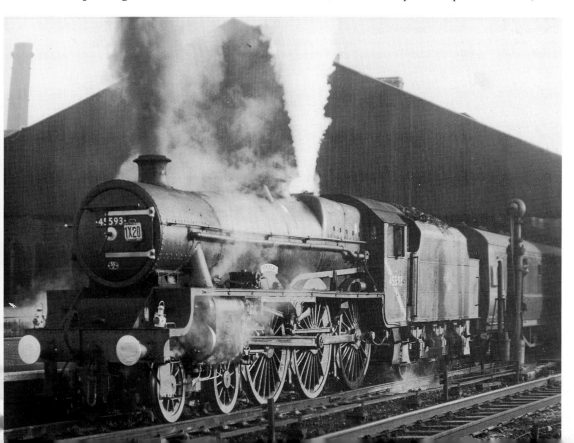

Above: Royston 8F No. 48281 passes Mirfield Up sidings with westbound special No. 1X12 on 19th August, 1961. The 8F was one of those with specially balanced driving wheels for working express freight trains which presumably made it suited to passenger work as well. *(Peter Rose)*

Trains requiring to leave the Up sidings and travel over the Single line towards the ground frame must not pass the "Stop Telephone" board situated near the connections between the sidings and the Single line until the guard has obtained the permission of the signalman at Healey Mills by means of the telephone provided on the stop board. *Eastern Region(Northern) Sectional Appendix 1975.*

Below: This strikingly atmospheric shot taken from Mirfield No.3 signal box shows Royal Scot 4-6-0 No. 46114 *Coldstream Guardsman* by-passing the station and crossing from the Down Fast to the Down Slow with a Liverpool Lime Street to Newcastle express in 1959. Speed signalling searchlight signals, including one of the few bracket types, are well in evidence while an 8F 2-8-0 and an ex-L&Y Aspinall 0-6-0 are busy in the Up yard on the left . *(Tony Ross)*

SHORT MEMORIES

4.7.66: The Newcastle-Red Bank vans is booked for diesel haulage from now on, usually a single York-based English Electric Type 4.

8.10.66: Preserved A3 4472 *Flying Scotsman* heads over Copy Pit with a Blackpool illuminations special from Lincolnshire.

Oct/Nov 1966: A diesel shortage sees the Red Bank vans steam again, usually pairs of Black Fives but on 9/11 by a single B1.

Nov 1966: Diesels start taking over Calder Valley freight work in some numbers following the allocation of English Electric Type 4s to the new Healey Mills depot.

Above: Inside Mirfield No.3 signal box, an L&Y box equipped with an LMS lever frame. It was abolished on 3rd May, 1970. *(Tony Ross)*

Below: Looking east at 2.50pm on 28th October, 1961. Wakefield-based Stanier 2-6-4T No. 42650 approaches Thornhill LNW Junction and passes Ravensthorpe station on the LNW Leeds line with the 2.22pm Saturdays Only Normanton-Sowerby Bridge local. Thornhill power station is on the left. *(David Holmes*

Above: Looking east towards Thornhill Junction, the station and its goods depots from Thornhill No. 1 signal box in 1961. The Heckmondwike branch comes in from the left. *(Stan Beat)*

The 1956 Railway Clearing House Handbook of Stations showed Thornhill as having a 5 ton yard crane and equipped to handle general goods, furniture vans, carriages, motor cars, portable engines, machines on wheels and livestock. Listed separately was Thornhill for Dewsbury which could handle horse boxes, prize cattle trucks, and carriages and motor cars by passenger and parcels train. Private sidings to the right of the above picture served J. Austin & Sons steel fabricators and stockholders, and Inghams Thornhill Colliery and coke ovens. Goods facilities were closed down in September, 1963 but the private sidings remained in operation for longer.

Below: Jubilee 4-6-0 No. 45698 *Mars* ignores Thornhill station - Thornhill for Dewsbury since 1930 - as it races by on the 10.30am Liverpool Exchange-Newcastle express during 1957. The impressive banner repeaters are for Thornhill No.2 home signals beyond the bridge. The tall lattice post carries Thornhill No.2 Down Fast starting signal with the Dewsbury West Junction Down Fast inner distant below. The signal on the right is the starter for Thornhill station east bay platform once used by Dewsbury Market Place trains. *(Tony Ross)*

Above: Thornhill for Dewsbury station in 1957 with BR Standard Class 3 2-6-0 No. 77001 on a Sowerby Bridge to Goole local. The east facing bay is on the left while at the opposite end of the platform occupied by the train was a west-facing bay still used at that time by the odd local train from Bradford. *(Tony Ross)*

Thornhill was originally intended to serve Dewsbury and was called Dewsbury to begin with. In summer 1957 it was served by regular trains to Bradford, Halifax, Manchester Victoria, Blackpool, Normanton, Goole and, on Saturdays, Scarborough.

It closed to passengers on 1st January, 1962 and in 1998 the only passenger trains on this part of the Calder Valley line, the hourly Wakefield-Liverpool Lime Street locals, pass by without stopping. Proposals by West Yorkshire PTE to open a new station at Thornhill have so far come to nothing.

Below: An unusual sight indeed on the L&Y main line in May, 1959. A diverted Bradford/Leeds to King's Cross express with A3 Pacific No. 60066 *Merry Hampton* in charge passes Dewsbury West Junction and the wagon works having travelled via Low Moor and Heckmondwike. The train has just passed under the huge bridge carrying the Midland line into Dewsbury Savile Town.

Top: Headfield Junction in 1954 with the lines to Dewsbury West Junction on the right and Dewsbury East Junction on the left. The ex-L&Y 0-6-0 is shunting the carriage and wagon works. The East spur remains a single track in 1998 and the west spur, severed in 1960, a siding into a cement depot on the site of the works. Part of the site is used by an industrial locomotive hire firm and various shunters are usually parked there. *(Tony Ross)*

Centre: Inside Dewsbury Junction shops on 3rd January, 1961. *(Fastline Photographic)*

Bottom: Class 4F 0-6-0 No. 44471 heads a short trip from Dewsbury Market Place past Headfield Junction in 1955. A spur to the GNR lines went through the bridge arch on the right. The plant on the right is Brown's chemical works. *(Tony Ross)*

Dewsbury C&W works consisted of a 9-road workshop, a 2-road wagon shed plus machine, joiners and other shops. It employed 60-70 people repairing and cleaning passenger and goods stock until 1961 when carriage cleaning and maintenance was switched to Low Moor and Wakefield. By the 1960s concern was gowing about the condition of the timber roof supports and the shops closed on 3rd June, 1967 when their workload was transferred to Wakefield engine shed which had itself just closed.

Dewsbury Market Place in 1955 with 4F 0-6-0 No. 44056 from Mirfield shed shunting one of the two daily trip workings. The west side of the yard on the left had just been lifted while the passenger station situated just in front and left of the distant town hall was long gone. *(Tony Ross)*

Dewsbury Market Place station consisted of two 100 yard platforms and central engine release road covered by an iron and glass trainshed roof, and a 42ft turntable. The two-storey buildings and concourse were across the northern end. In 1910 it saw 19 weekday trains to and 16 from Thornhill, three to(four on Sats) and two from(three on Sats) Wakefield. First arrival was the 5.12am from Wakefield and first departure the 5.20 to Thornhill. Last train was the 10.10pm from Thornhill. The station closed in 1930 and was demolished in 1938/9, the site being used for road improvements.

Goods facilities included a two-road goods warehouse, a large two-road shoddy warehouse and two single-road shoddy sheds all with internal cranes plus coal depots, stables, loading docks, and a 5-ton yard crane. Outward traffic once included nightsoil and during the first world war it was a major depot for army great coats. In 1954 the west side of the yard was sold to become a swimming pool and council offices. The rest closed in 1961 and is now occupied by a leisure centre, supermarket and car parks.

── DEWSBURY MARKET PLACE FROM A 1907 1/2500 MAP ──
By courtesy of the Ordnance Survey

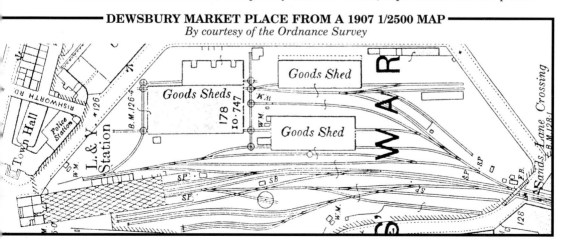

SHORT MEMORIES

5.11.66: The Bradford-Stockport service is withdrawn. Fairburn 2-6-4T 42116 with a headboard hauls the last train.

March, 1967: One of the last regular steam passenger trains in West Yorkshire is the 2.10am York-Manchester Victoria west of Normanton. An Eastern Region loco works it to Halifax where it reverses and an LM Region Class 5 takes over.

June 1967: About half the Calder Valley freights are still hauled by LMR steam locos.

9.6.67: The 17.34 FO Manchester Exchange-York, one of the last Trans-Pennine steam trains, is switched to the Calder Valley, leaving Manchester Exchange at 17.47. On this day it is powered by Carlisle Britannia 4-6-2 70035 *Rudyard Kipling*.

Above: Dewsbury East Junction looking towards Thornhill Midland Junction in 1961. The freight train is stopped at Midland Junction's home signal. The Market Place branch comes in from the left, the siding following it being used to store empty wagons from the nearby gas works or stock awaiting attention at the wagon works. *(Stan Beat)*

Until the end of the 1950s the Dewsbury East - Headfield line served Dewsbury gasworks and Brown's chemical works. The gasworks received coal which once came from the GN via the Headfield curve as well as the L&Y. Brown's, whose sidings were connected to Headfield Junction, produced tar acid and sulphuric acid which left by rail in their own tank wagons.

Below: It is a summer evening in 1960 and Jubilee No. 45698 *Mars* makes a fine sight amid the semaphore signals as it forges west past Thornhill Midland Junction with the 5.10pm Newcastle to Liverpool Exchange express. The Midland line from Middlestown Junction comes down the bank on the right. *(Tony Ross)*

Above: A Jubilee heads a June, 1962 summer Saturday excursion from Sheffield along the Midland line from Royston between the flying Middlestown Junction(in the background) and Thornhill Midland Junction where it will join the L&Y line for its journey to Blackpool. Stored wagons line the Savile Town branch on the right.

Right: The end of the line for the Midland. Still in LMS colours around 1950, 70 year-old 2F 0-6-0 22975(BR 58154) shunts the daily trip from Carlton at Dewsbury Goods Junction, just before the drop into Savile Town. *(Tony Ross)*

Below: Back on the L&Y, Fairburn tank No. 42094 passes the old Healey Mills yard and approaches Healey Mills West signal box with the 5.23pm York to Manchester Victoria express in summer, 1959. After Wakefield, this notable fast train stopped only at Sowerby Bridge, Todmorden and Rochdale before Manchester. *(Tony Ross)*

Above: Heckmondwike was where the L&Y line from the Calder Valley main line at Thornhill joined the West Riding Union Mirfield-Low Moor line. Besides its local service the line was once used by some main line trains, regular excursions and occasional diversions. With the goods depot on the right and the station behind, Jubilee No. 45694 *Bellerophon* departs Heckmondwike with the 9.23am guarenteed excursion to Blackpool on 16th May, 1964. *(David Holmes)*
The station closed on 14th June, 1965 but goods facilities lasted until May, 1969.

THE WEST RIDING UNION & HALIFAX

HECKMONDWIKE PASSENGER TRAIN DEPARTURES SUMMER 1957

6.44am	6.23	Bradford-Huddersfield	6.39am	6am	Huddersfield-Bradford
7.29am	7.10	Bradford-Huddersfield	7.36am	7.32	Thornhill-Bradford
7.59am	7.40	Bradford-Huddersfield	7.52amSX	7.35	Huddersfield-Bradford
8.54am	8.35	Bradford-Huddersfield	8.20am	7.23	Penistone-Bradford
10.10amSO	9.35	Sowerby Bridge-Scarborough	8.30amSO	8.5	Wakefield-Blackburn 22/6,29/6,6/7
11.56amSO	11.37	Bradford-Huddersfield	8.51am	7.57	Knottingley-Bradford
12.55pm	12.33	Bradford-Huddersfield	11.3am	10.15	Penistone-Bradford
4.16pm SO/4.19SX	1.30	Blackpool-Wakefield	12.51pm	12.33	Huddersfield-Bradford
4.28pm	4.5	Bradford-Penistone	1.1pm	12.40	Wakefield-Bradford
5.10pm SX	5.4	Cleckheaton-Penistone	2.27pmSO	2.10	Huddersfield-Bradford
5.24pm	5.5	Bradford-Thornhill	3.33pmSO	12.25	Scarborough-Sowerby Bridge
6.2pm	5.40	Bradford-Huddersfield	3.59pm	3.40	Wakefield-Bradford
6.37pm	6.15	Bradford-Wakefield	4.7pmSX	4.0	Mirfield-Cleckheaton
7.20pm	6.59	Bradford-Huddersfield	4.50pm	4.33	Huddersfield-Bradford
9.46pm SO	9.27	Bradford-Huddersfield	5.49pm	5.5	Holmfirth-Bradford
10.5pm SO	9.45	Bradford-Goole	5.56pm	4.30	Goole-Bradford
10.39pm	10.20	Bradford-Huddersfield	8.10pm	7.52	Huddersfield-Bradford
11.26pmSO	11.7	Bradford-Huddersfield	9.32pm	9.10	Huddersfield-Bradford

HECKMONDWIKE CURVE: The line is worked under the regulations for working single lines by One Train Only ... but no Train Staff is provided. Trains may be worked with a locomotive at each end. When a train is worked by two locomotives to Liversedge(oil terminal) both locomotives must return with the train. *BR Eastern Region(Northern) Sectional Appendix, 1975.*

Above: B1 4-6-0 No. 61016 *Inyala* - less nameplates - makes a spectacular start from Cleckheaton with an eastbound 1960s excursion. The passenger station consisted of just an island platform but there was an array of goods and shoddy warehouses. Like Heckmondwike and Liversedge, this station was named Central from 1924 to 61 and closed on 14th June, 1965. *(N. E. Stead collection)*

Below: A Fowler 2-6-4T threads its way between the busy, rambling Cleckheaton goods yards while leaving Central station with a Bradford-bound stopping train in 1957. The picture shows shoddy warehouses on the left and right with the general goods depot and its 10-ton yard crane immediately left of the main line. A loading dock and coal yard are on the right while a WD 2-8-0 stands in the sidings on the left. All this was wiped out in May, 1969 when the goods facilities closed and one cannot help but wonder where all this traffic went to.

Above: Despite having Starbeck on its buffer beam, J39 0-6-0 64859 was a Mirfield engine, just transferred from West Auckland when photographed at Cleckheaton while working the morning trip to Ellison's Sidings on 26th April, 1962. *(Robert Anderson)*

BOOKED SPEN VALLEY LINE FREIGHT WORKINGS 2.11.59-2.6.60

Down direction

2.45am MX Wakefield-Bradford Goods class K
3.38am Mirfield-Low Moor class F
5.30am Mirfield-Cleckheaton class K
5.50am Mirfield -Cleckheaton class K
9.2am   Heckmondwike-Low Moor class K
LM34 Trip
9.35am Cleckheaton-Low Moor class K
2.50am Brewery Sidings-Low Moor class K
1.15pm SX Thornhill-Low Moor class K
2.33pm SX Mirfield-Heckmondwike engine &
brake van
3pm SX Heckmondwike-Cleckheaton light engine
3.30pm SX Cleckheaton-Ellison's Siding class K
6.12pm SX Heckmondwike-Healey Mills class H
6.20 pmSX Cleckheaton-Hillhouse class E
6.25pm SX Mirfield-Cleckheaton engine & brake
7.20pm SX Cleckheaton-Carlton class H
via Low Moor
7.35pm SX Cleckheaton-Low Moor class H
6.30pm SX Crofton West-Bradford Goods class H
11.15pmSX Mirfield-Laisterdyke class D

Up direction

6.10am Low Moor-Heckmondwike class K
LM34 Trip
8.27am Cleckheaton-Heckmondwike class K
9.5am Heckmondwike-Mirfield engine and
brake van
10.30am Ellison's Siding-Cleckheaton class K
12.15pm SX Bradford Goods-Healey Mills class K
LM36 Trip
3.50pm SX Ellison's Siding-Cleckheaton class K
4.30pm SO Cleckheaton-Mirfield class K
4.36pm SX Low Moor-Heckmondwike
light engine
5.25pm SX Low Moor-Cleckheaton class F
6.28pm SO Low Moor-Wakefield Witham's
Sidings class F
7.10pm SX Low Moor-Cleckheaton engine &
brake van
8.15pm SX Cleckheaton-Mirfield class H
7.35pm SX Bradford Goods-Hillhouse class E
9.30pm SX Bradford Goods-Longwood class E
9.45pm SX Bradford Goods-Healey Mills class H

Trains to be shunted into Down Through Siding at Cleckheaton box: When a freight train is to be shunted into the Down Through Siding the guard, before giving the driver a hand signal to set back, must pin down enough wagon brakes at the rear of the train to prevent, in the event of a breakloose, the rear portion running back. *BR Eastern Region(Northern) Sectional Appendix, 1968.*

Above: Back to the diversions of spring, 1959. On 12th April, A1 Pacific No. 60123 *H. A. Ivatt* graces the Spen Valley line while passing Ellison's tar works and Ellison's Siding signal box with the Harrogate Sunday Pullman. *(D. Butterfield / N. E. Stead collection)*

Below: On the same day another A1, this time No. 60125 *Scottish Union,* has just left Low Moor and is near Oakenshaw with the diverted Sunday 1.12pm Leeds to King's Cross. .

Above: The Low Moor south curve, approaching from the right, provided direct access between Halifax, the Spen Valley and beyond until being abandoned in 1981. With the carriage sidings on its right, Jubilee 4-6-0 No. 45565 *Victoria* gets going with the 11.5am Low Moor-Blackpool, formed of non-corridor coaches, on Whit Monday 3rd June,1963. *(Robert Anderson)*

Full coverage of this once important railway centre is given in Railway Memories No 4.

In winter 1959/60 the Low Moor Halifax - Greetland Milner Royd line carried 19 booked westbound and 16 eastbound freights on weekdays, plus light engines and trips between Greetland and the Halifax High Level. They included two Halifax-Ardsley Wrenthorpe and three Ardsley Halifax/North Bridge workings. A one-off which ran when required was the 9.24am from Low Moor taking engines to Horwich Works. Needless to say, the line carries no freight at all in 1998.

Above: Black Five No. 45208 passes Low Moor No.1 signal box and heads for Halifax with the 11.40 Bradford-Belle Vue excursion on Whit Monday, 1963. Low Moor turned out 15 4-6-0s for special traffic on this day, 14 spotless Black Fives and a dirty B1. *(Robert Anderson)*

Top: The first station after Low Moor was Wyke and Norwood Green, pictured in the early 1900s looking north towards the 1,365-yard Wyke Tunnel. Replacing the earlier Pickle Bridge station in 1882, it closed to passengers in 1953 and goods in 1964.

Right: One of just two stations on the Brighouse line was Bailiff Bridge, seen here in L&Y days with an 0-6-0 on a stopping train. The timber station was devastated by fire in 1917 and never reopened.
(Both Lens of Sutton)

Left: The Pickle Bridge line was the most direct Bradford-Huddersfield route and in 1910 carried 18 Down and 20 Up weekday passenger trains, including Marylebone expresses.

This was how it ended its days. The pile-up was at Wakefield Road, Wyke, on 25th July, 1952, the year of its complete closure.
(Arthur Wilson)

Above: A London and North Western infiltrator and a timely reminder that for a year the L&Y system was under the control of its rival, the LNWR. In 1938, LNW design G2a Class 0-8-0 No. 9004 powers a Bradford-bound goods through Lightcliffe station. *(Locofotos))*

Left: Lightcliffe station on 4th April 1964 with a Huddersfield to Bradford Metro-Cammel DMU in the platform. The station's last passenger train was the 5.44pm from Bradford on 12th June, 1965 and it was demolished in 1966. Goods traffic lasted until 1967 but in 1998 nothing remained except the station house on the left. Spot the white lion. *(Jack Wild/S. Chapman collection)*

In 1946 there were 13 direct Leeds-Halifax trains each weekday and 14 from Leeds avoiding Bradford. Nowadays the only way is by going in and out of Bradford.

On Whit Monday 11th June, 1962 BR ran an excursion from Low Moor to Blackpool calling at Lightcliffe(8.25am, returning 8pm) Sowerby Bridge and Hebden Bridge. The adult return fare from Lightcliffe was 13s 6d(67.5p).

Right: Near Lightcliffe was the works of Brookes Ltd., suppliers of paving stones to over 500 local authorities and famous for non-slip concrete slabs.

They once had eight miles of internal railway connecting the works with quarries and the main line exchange sidings. There were some steep gradients, like the 1 in 14 down from the works to the exchange sidings. By the early 1960s the system had been reduced to four miles.

The longest stretch of track by then ran from the works to an aerial ropeway at Broad Oak, alongside the A644 Halifax-Brighouse road. The ropeway brought coal and fireclay from Waterclough Colliery, the coal being used to fire the brickworks.

Brookes had three locomotives, two Peckett 0-6-0STs, *Silex No.2* built 1931, *Nonslip Stone*, built 1956, and Hunslet 0-6-0ST *Brookes No.1*, built 1941. One of the Pecketts is pictured inside the two-road engine shed during 1956.

The works closed in 1969 after 130 years' production. The Pecketts were scrapped on site but the Hunslet was saved and in 1997 was at the Middleton Railway, Leeds.

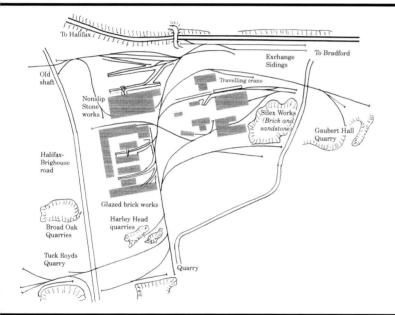

Below: Between Lightcliffe and Halifax was Hipperholme station, pictured looking towards the 388-yard Hipperholme Tunnel in L&Y days.

Back in 1946 Hipperholme was served by eight weekday trains to Halifax and nine direct to Leeds but by June 1953 was closed to passengers and to goods in April, 1966. Very little is left to see in 1998.

(Lens of Sutton)

Above: Brookes railway as it was around 1915.
Not to scale)

After closure, the whole works was auctioned off along with the locomotives. The site is now occupied by Europe's biggest tumble dryer factory.

Above: On 19th August, 1936, L&Y 0-6-0 No.12104, one of those rebuilt with an extended smokebox and Belpaire firebox, jumped the points at Hipperholme goods yard, blocking the main line and requiring assistance from another, unrebuilt member of the class. The cottage in the background was demolished in 1997.
(Arthur Wilson / A. Whitaker collection)

Below: On 8th October, 1966 the Locomotive Club of Great Britain ran a Liverpool-Goole railtour hauled as far as Wakefield by "Crab" No. 42942. The special is seen crossing Shibden Dale on its way from Halifax towards the Spen Valley line. *(Robert Anderson)*

SHORT MEMORIES

Nov 1967: Calderdale hosts West Yorkshire's last regular steam passenger trains - the 17.47FO Man Exchange-York(steam as far as Normanton), 03.10 MO Normanton-Halifax (engine off the 17.47), 03.32 Leeds-Halifax and the 04.38 Halifax Manchester Victoria. The 17.47 is still often a Britannia Pacific.

Nov 1967: Single Class 47 diesels take over Stanlow-Leeds oil trains from double-headed steam, often 9F 2-10-0s.

20.5.68: The 03.32MX Leeds-Halifax and 04.38 Halifax-Manchester Vic become diesel.

June, 1968: Just 8 daily steam-hauled freights left on the Calder Valley.

Left: Looking east from platform three at Halifax station in December, 1966. Halifax East signal box is on the left while one of the BR Standard Class 5 4-6-0s with Caprotti valve gear, No. 73137, backs on to its train in platform two. *(Jack Wild / Stephen Chapman collection).*

Below; The north end of Halifax station looking towards the 1,105-yard Beacon Hill Tunnel on 22nd January, 1971. The connections onto the GN side have been removed along with the platform three road but track over the viaduct to North Bridge remains in use, being accessed via South Parade goods yard. Track has gone from the covered loading dock serving Patons and Baldwins textiles, neighbouring Riding Hall Carpets mill dominates the background, while the three lines on the left of the picture go to the large coal drops which are preserved to this day. *(Fastline Photographic)*

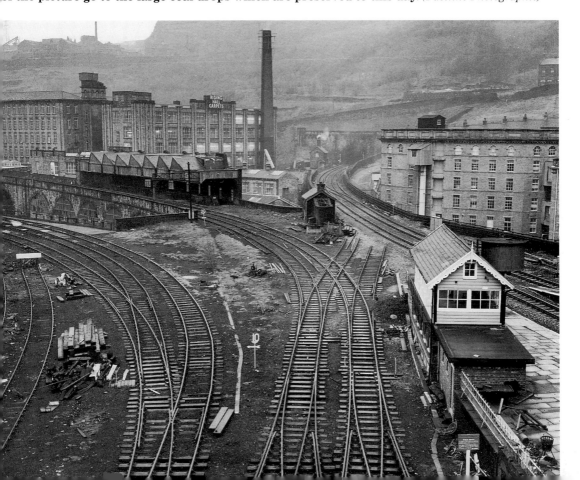

Above: Stanier 2-6-4T No. 42664 has assisted Jubilee No. 45581 *Bihar and Orissa* up the steep climb from Greetland with the Poole to Bradford train on 16th July, 1966. The pair stand by Halifax East box at 7.50pm while awaiting departure from platform three. *(Robert Anderson)*

Left: B1 4-6-0 No. 61022 *Sassaby* waits to leave the same platform with a Bradford express in September, 1965. This once busy platform remains a trackless eyesore in 1998. *(Jack Wild / Stephen Chapman collection)* Halifax Old was renamed Halifax Town in 1951, becoming just Halifax in 1961.

In 1957 the intermediate signal boxes between Milner Royd and Low Moor were Dryclough Junction, Holdsworth Bridge, Halifax West, Halifax Goods Yard, Halifax East, Hipperholme, Lightcliffe, and Wyke. Maximum speed on the Up and Down main lines in 1968 was 60mph Milner Royd-Halifax West, 30mph through Halifax station, 40/45mph Halifax East-Lightcliffe and 55mph from there onwards.

Signalling was Absolute Block on the main lines. There were two additional Goods lines on the Down side as far as Halifax East(controlled by Halifax Goods Yard box) one starting at Holdsworth Bridge, the other at Halifax West, and one on the Up side from Halifax East to West, all being Permissive Block. There were also one additional Up and two additional Down passenger lines through the station.

A train still dividing at Halifax in the 1960s was the 11.30 Blackpool to Wakefield and Bradford, seen there on 2nd August, 1961. Crewe North Black Five No. 44764 awaits its 4pm departure from platform three with the Wakefield portion while Fowler 2-6-4T No. 42310 will take the Bradford portion out five minutes later. Nowadays, only the island platform on the right is used. *(Peter Rose)*

Jack Wild knew the railways of Halifax as well as anyone, having studied them since the 1930s.

"Halifax Old station was a very busy railway centre then, jointly run by the LNER and LMS.

"Platforms 1 and 2 were an island with waiting rooms, 3 and 4 comprised the main building, No. 4 on the north side being where the main entrance used to be. Both had access to first class Ladies and Gentlemen's waiting rooms, station master's office, refreshment rooms, telegraph office and a large, busy parcels office. Platforms 5 and 6, also an island with waiting and refreshment rooms and a staff canteen, were on a tight curve.

"LNER trains, including through coaches for London - on the 10.15 via Queensbury - used 5 and 6 and LMS trains for Leeds and Bradford No. 3. LMS trains for Manchester, the West, and local trains, used 1 and 2.

"Decorative white ceramic finger plates on the Gents lavatory doors advised their clientel to visit the "Renowned Dome Room Grill when visiting Victoria station in Manchester."

"There were three sizeable goods yards, coal and wagonload sidings, a cattle dock and the coal drops down to road level. An electric overhead travelling crane stood over one siding and hand cranes in the yard alongside the large warehouse.

"Freight consisted mainly of coal but there was considerable container traffic while heavy engineering products and machines were catered for by the overhead crane. Patons and Baldwins had a private covered siding on the LNER line for worsted and knitting wool from Bailey Hall Mills.

Mackintosh's sent traffic from their chocolate and toffee factory at Albion Mills.

"The LMS had a big "Latil" tractor and low loader for carrying heavy machinery such as lathes and planing machines from Asquith's and Butler's, the machine tool makers.

"Parcels were collected and delivered by short tail 4-wheel horse vans later superseded by 3-wheel Karrier Cobs and then by Scammel mechanical horses. For many years after the second world war, goods around the town centre were carried by heavy, black LMS 4-wheel wagons. It had about 12 horses stabled at the junction of Prescott Street and South Parade. The LNER had a smaller number at South Parade goods yard.

"Many local LMS services to Leeds, Manchester and beyond were then operated by ex-Midland 2P 4-4-0s while local trains were in the hands of ex-L&Y 2-4-2Ts. Locos on the LNER branch were chiefly the Gresley N1 0-6-2Ts but ex-Great Central types made frequent appearances. The LNER used teak articulated coaches which I believe came from the London area. Goods engines included the ex-L&Y 0-6-0s and Fowler large boilered 0-8-0s nicknamed "Baby Austins" or "Elephant and Soap Boxes." Ex-L&Y 0-6-0STs from Sowerby Bridge did the shunting.

"Nowadays, Halifax station is but a shadow of its old self. Only platforms 1 and 2 are used and platform 3 is a perfect eyesore. All goods facilities have gone."

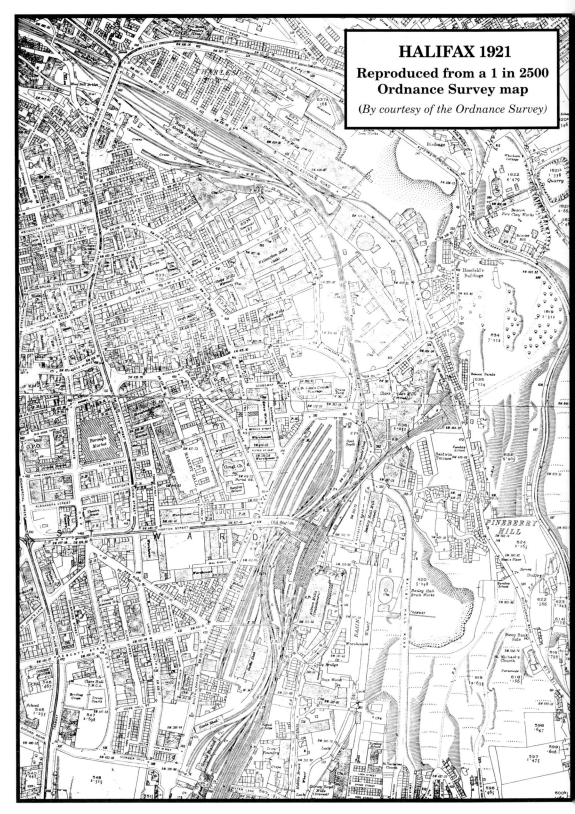

HALIFAX 1921

Reproduced from a 1 in 2500
Ordnance Survey map

(*By courtesy of the Ordnance Survey*)

Top: Fairburn 2-6-4T No. 42141 stands in platform two with an evening parcels train in August, 1965.

Centre: Platform three back in August, 1968, complete with intact roof, signs, various waiting rooms, a wooden wheel barrow and the clock at half past four.

Bottom: The well-covered 1880s entrance to Halifax station in August, 1968. The canopies were eventually done away with and the whole lot left open to the elements, though a much smaller modern canopy was erected in the 1980s. In this scene the cars and parcels delivery vans are as interesting as the railway element. The cars are parked on the bridge carrying the entrance over the GN platforms and sidings. (All Jack Wild/Stephen Chapman collection)

HALIFAX TOWN PASSENGER SERVICES, WEEKDAYS, SUMMER 1957

Departure times shown except in the case of terminating trains where arrival times are shown

TIME	TRAIN
am	
4.8	3.25 Leeds Central-Manchester Vic.
4.23	3.15 Normanton-Manchester Vic *Reverses*
5.42	5.21 Bradford-Penistone
6.54	6.32 Bradford-Liverpool Exchange
7.25SO	To Leeds City via Greetland, Elland, and Brighouse *29/6-31/8*
7.40	7.15 Bradford-Manchester Vic.
7.45	7.22 Bradford-Penistone
7.58	7.35 Bradford-Stockport.
8.28SX/8.23 SO	8.5 Bradford-Huddersfield
8.40	7.55 Leeds/8.15Bradford-Liverpool Ex.
8.45	To Stockport
8.58SO	8.5 Wakefield-Cleckheaton-Blackpool Central *22.6/29.6/6.7*
9.8	8.24 Leeds/8.45 Bradford-Blackpool
9.38	8.55 Leeds/9.15 Bradford-Liverpool Ex.
9.58 SO	9.30 Bradford-Blackpool *13.7-31.8*
10.11SO	9.45 Bradford-Llandudno
10.16	10am Bradford-Marylebone *The South Yorkshireman*
10.32SO	10.15 Bradford-Poole
11.40	10.55 Leeds/11.15 Bradford-Liverpool Ex.
pm	
12.7 SO	All stations to Huddersfield
12.33/12.23 SO	12.10 Bradford-Sowerby Bridge
12.35SO	11.55 Leeds/12.15 Bradford-Manchester
1.40	12.55 Leeds/1.15 Bradford-Liverpool Ex.
1.53	1.32 Bradford- Penistone
2.40SX	1.55Leeds/2.15 Bradford-Liverpool Ex.
3.18	2.55 Bradford-Penistone
3.55	To Stockport
4.7 SO	12.25 Scarborough-Sowerby Bridge
4.39	3.55 Leeds/ 4.15 Bradford SX-Manchester SO/Liverpool SX
4.42 SX	To Manchester Victoria
4.51	4.28 Bradford-Holmfirth
5.12 SX	To Todmorden
5.26	4.50 Bradford-Huddersfield/Holmfirth SX
5.46	5.10Leeds/5.15 Bradford-Liverpool Exch. *Combines at Halifax*
5.56	5.35 Bradford-Huddersfield
6.5	To Manchester Victoria
6.51	6.27 Bradford-Clayton West
7.42	6.55 Leeds/7.15 Bradford-Southport
8.11	7.47 Bradford-Huddersfield
8.32 SO	3.18 from King's Cross via Bradford
9.37	8.50 Leeds Central-Manchester Vic.
10.25	9.55 Bradford-Huddersfield
10.56SO	10.16 Leeds Central-Manchester Vic.
11.17SX	6.15 from King's Cross via Bradford
11.24	10.45 Leeds-Sowerby Bridge

TIME	TRAIN
am	
4.10	3.15 from Normanton
6.8	5.58 Sowerby Bridge-Bradford
6.59	6.23 Huddersfield-Bradford
7.34	6.15 Clayton West-Low Moor
7.46	6.15 Manchester Vic.-Bradford
8.12	7.42 from Holmfirth
8.26SX	8.17 Sowerby Bridge-Leeds Central
9.0 SX	To London King's Cross via Bradford
9.14	7am Southport-Leeds & Bradford
9.44 SO	9.35 Sowerby Bridge-Scarborough *Until 24/8* Via Cleckheaton
10.3 SO	To London King's Cross via Bradford
10.23	8.30 Liverpool Ex.-Leeds & Bradford
10.40	9.30 Penistone-Bradford
11.31 SX	9.40 Liverpool Ex.-Leeds & Bradford
11.51 SO	8.5 Llandudno-Bradford
pm	
12.10 SO	12.0 Sowerby Bridge-Bradford
12.58	12.13 Huddersfield-Bradford
1.16SO	11.47 Bolton-Leeds
1.27	11.30 Liverpool Ex.-Leeds & Bradford
1.41SO	11.5am Blackpool-Bradford *From 13/7*
2.43	12.30 Liverpool Ex.-Leeds & Bradford
3.0 SX	1.42 Stockport-Bradford
3.10	1.0 Southport-Leeds & Bradford
3.27SO	1.30 Liverpool Ex.-Bradford *Until 17/8*
3.34	2.40 Penistone-Bradford
3.41 SO	2.25 Stockport-Bradford
3.46 SO	1.20 Blackpool-Leeds & Bradford
3.57 SO	1.10 Blackpool-Cleckheaton-Wakefield
4.0/4.5 SX	1.30 Blackpool-Wakefield & Bradford
4.6	2.42 from Manchester Vic.
4.33	2.30 Liverpool Ex.-Leeds & Bradford
5.3 SX	4.55 Sowerby Bridge-Bradford
5.28	3.30 Liverpool Ex.-Leeds & Bradford
5.39	5.8 Huddersfield-Bradford
5.53	4.37 from Manchester Vic.
6.24	4.30 Liverpool Ex.-Leeds & Bradford
6.32	5.15 Penistone-Bradford
6.37SX	6.10 from Todmorden
7.0 SO	10.25am Poole-Bradford
7.28	6.20 Penistone-Bradford
8.7	6.45 Manchester Vic.-Bradford
8.38	8.30 Sowerby Bridge-Bradford
9.1	7.28 Stockport-Bradford
9.13	7.48 Manchester Vic.-Leeds Central
9.38SX	7.30 Blackpool-Leeds & Bradford
9.45SO	8.35 Manchester Vic.-Bradford
10.4	4.50 London Marylebone-Bradford *The South Yorkshireman*
10.46	9.30 Penistone-Bradford
11.2	8.30 Liverpool Ex.-Leeds & Bradford

Above: A magnifying glass may be necessary to see the detail in this view taken from Beacon Hill in 1956. A westbound 2-6-4T is leaving the station while another tank engine stands at the east end and an L&Y 0-6-0 shunts the former GN goods yard with its multi-storey warehouse and travelling crane. Church Street coal yard, in front of the church, is full of wagons. Behind the church is the famous Piece Hall and somewhere up on the murky horizon peppered with mill chimneys is the High Level line. The Eureka children's interactive museum now occupies the site of the GN yard.

Left: The LNER curiously named new B17 Footballer 4-6-0 No. 2871 *Manchester City* in Halifax, not Manchester. The ceremony is seen taking place on 11th June, 1937 with the mayor and schoolchildren present at the west end of platform 4. The LMS named Royal Scot No. 6145 *The Duke of Wellington's Regiment* in a military ceremony at the station on 4th October, 1936. *(Arthur Wilson / A. Whitaker colln.)*

Right: Halifax West signal box looking towards the L&Y goods yard in 1968. The GN(right) and L&Y warehouses still stand, disused, in 1998. A 204hp diesel shunter is in the L&Y yard but in the 1990s only one siding is used, as a turnback for Leeds-Halifax diesel units. *(Jack Wild / Stephen Chapman collection)*

Above: The pride of the line between 1948 and 1960 was the South Yorkshireman to London Marylebone. In 1957 it left Bradford at 10am and called at Halifax, Brighouse, Huddersfield, Brockholes and Shepley & Shelley(if required), Denby Dale, Sheffield Victoria, Nottingham Victoria, Loughborough, Leicester, Rugby, and Aylesbury, arriving Marylebone at 3.37pm. The return service left Marylebone at 4.50pm, reaching Halifax at 10.4pm. Thus in those days, Halifax not only had through London expresses but a direct East Midlands service as well.

Here, the London-bound train passes Holdsworth Bridge signal box in June, 1958 hauled by B1 4-6-0 No. 61319. The former L&Y goods depots behind stand near the old Shaw Syke station. With all goods facilities closed in 1981, the shed shown has been replaced by a retail warehouse.

Below: One summer's afternoon in 1964, a Fairburn 2-6-4T takes the Greetland line at Dryclough Junction with the 3.58pm Halifax-Stockport express, complete with Palethorpe's sausage van bringing up the rear. The line to Milner Royd and Manchester is in the foreground. The Greetland line was closed and mothballed in 1988 but by the year 2000 it could hopefully be carrying a reinstated Bradford-Huddersfield service. *(Jack Wild)*

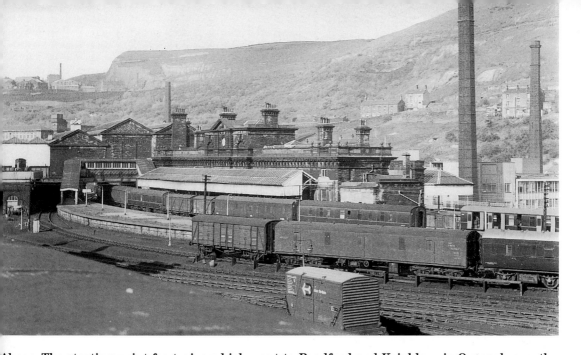

Above: The starting point for trains which went to Bradford and Keighley via Queensbury - the GN platforms at Halifax in summer, 1966. Platforms 5 and 6, disused and devoid of buildings since 1958, are nearest while platform 4 is busy with parcels traffic. *(Jack Wild / S. Chapman collection)*

OVER THE ALPS

Below: It is 1947 and the LNER and LMS are on their way out, to be replaced by the nationalised British Railways, though you wouldn't know it from this scene. LNER apple green B1 4-6-0 No. 1268 backs onto an excursion beneath the station entrance at the east end of platform 5. *(Jack Wild collection)*

In 1946 weekday trains left Halifax Old for Keighley at 5.34, 6.35, 7.50, 9.1, and 10.12am, 3.35, 4.45, 6.45 and 9.10pm. They left for Bradford at 8.20, 11.45am, 12.3, 1.17, 4.23, 5.10, 5.43, 7.50 and 10.25pm, and most took 32 minutes. The 11.45 stopped only at North Bridge and Holmfield, took 25 minutes and conveyed through carriages for King's Cross which returned by the 11.22pm arrival which ran non-stop from Bradford in 22 minutes. The London portion was the only Sunday train.

Above: The Queensbury lines are best remembered for local passenger trains hauled by ex-GN N1 0-6-2Ts but they also carried through freight traffic. Here, a heavy Through Freight hauled by LNER B1 No. 1229 passes Halifax gas works, and its long, curving shed where coal was received, on its way between Old and North Bridge stations during the late 1940s. It will soon be struggling over the Alps to Laisterdyke or Ardsley yards. *(Jack Wild collection)*

Left: This very basic overhead electric locomotive, which appears to have been converted from a wagon and is pictured in 1948, was used for moving wagons along a tramway between the main line and the gas works. *(Arthur Wilson)*

HALIFAX CORPORATION GAS WORKS: Overhead electrical wires are erected over the sidings at these works. A railway locomotive must not be allowed to enter the sidings until the current has been cut off by the Corporation staff, and the indicator, which is placed at the entrance to the sidings, about 30 yards from North Bridge South signal box, is at the "All Clear" position. When the electric current is on, the disc indicates "Warning - Live Wires." *BR N.E. Region Sectional Appendix, 1960.*

HIGH LEVEL LINE BOOKED FREIGHT SERVICES WINTER 1959/60

	A		SX	SX	SO	
Greetland dep				11.5	11.20	2.15pm
Halifax Goods SB	6.4am	6.35	10.40	11.21	11.36	2.33
North Bridge arr		6.40	10.45	11.25	11.40	2.37
North Bridge dep	6.23			11.37		2.40
Holmfield arr	6.40			11.54		3.15
Holmfield dep	6.45			12.9pm		3.50
Pellon arr	6.57			12.24		4.5
Pellon dep	7.7			12.34		4.15
St. Paul's arr	7.12			12.39		4.20

		D	B		C	
St. Paul's dep	7.50		12.49		4.30	
Pellon arr	7.55		12.54	1.14	4.35	
Pellon dep	9.5			1.20	4.50	
Holmfield arr	9.15			1.22	5.0	
Holmfield dep	10.5				5.30	
North Bridge arr	10.17				5.40	
North Bridge dep		10.27			5.55	7.5
Halifax Goods SB		10.32		1.32	6.0	7.10
Greetland arr				1.45		

A: 5.5am from Brighouse (Sowerby Bridge 33 Trip - "The Klondyke Special")

B: Engine and brake van

C: Empties to Crofton Hall

D: Light engine to Greetland. Off 7.50am from St. Paul's.

All trains were class J

> "Main line trains left wagons for the High Level at 'High Level' sidings, Greetland, where Sowerby Bridge engines collected them.
> "In the quiet early morning you could hear the first train leave Greetland and struggle against greasy rails all the way up through Halifax, Ovenden and Pellon," *Jack Wild.*

Through freight trains using the Queensbury line, all operated by the LNER, in the 1930s consisted of mid-morning and mid-afternoon Halifax-Ardsley class Ds, a class B express goods from Halifax at about 5pm and two late night class Ds to Bradford. Coming to Halifax was a mid-morning class B from Ardsley, a mid-afternoon class D from Laisterdyke, an afternoon cattle train from Clayton which ran when required and an evening class D from Laisterdyke. Most of these trains stopped to pick up and drop off High Level line wagons at Holmfield. One of the evening trains from Halifax was nicknamed the 'Toffee Special' because it carried traffic from Mackintosh's.

Below: Big LMS Fowler 7F 0-8-0 No. 49592 shunts by the Central Electricity Authority power station at the south end of North Bridge goods yard in June, 1956. By then this sizeable yard was handling wagonload goods and mineral traffic only. Used for rail traffic until 1974, the site is now occupied by a leisure centre, a supermarket and car parks.

Left: The non too grand entrance to North Bridge station in the 1950s. The purpose of the "danger" notice is intriguing.

The North Bridge itself was built as part of the construction of the Halifax and Ovenden Joint line, replacing an old stone bridge.

The mostly timber station buildings were demolished in May, 1960.

Below: A murky yet fascinating view of North Bridge station from the bridge itself in December, 1948 with B1 4-6-0s 61309 and 61082 present. Just beyond them is the unusually shaped signal box. *(Arthur Wilson)*

On Sunday 30th July, 1939, the LNER ran a half-day excursion of corridor stock from Halifax Old to Bridlington. It left Old station at 10.45am and North Bridge at 10.49, Ovenden 10.54 and reached Queensbury at 11am where it combined with a portion from Keighley. It continued via Bradford, Morley Top, Ardsley and Castleford and was due back to Halifax Old at 11.38pm. Arrangements were made for Halifax Corporation buses to take trippers home. The return 3rd class fare was 4s 9d. With war looming there would be few more excursions for the next six years.

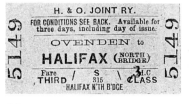

Above: A long-lost Halifax scene to delight enthusiasts but probably one which would not be allowed nowadays. Class C12 4-4-2T No. 4536, of Great Northern origin, prepares to make a smoky departure from North Bridge with a pair of creaky old wooden coaches for the Queensbury line in June, 1939. After the war, No. 4536 was renumbered 7386, becoming BR 67386.

Below: Under the North Bridge itself , an ex-L&Y Aspinall 3F 0-6-0, LMS No.12237, shunts the goods yard. North Bridge closed to goods in 1964 but continued as a coal yard until 1st April, 1974, after which the remaining track and facilities were abandoned along with the line from Halifax station. *(Both Jack Wild collection)*

Above: The site of North Bridge station in February 1964. One track remains providing access to the goods yard. The large buildings are the Dean Clough Mills of Crossley's Carpets which were connected to the main line by a steeply-graded branch dropping away from just under the footbridge and then passing under the main line into the mill complex. *(Jack Wild/Stephen Chapman collection)*

Below: Class N1 0-6-2T No. 69464 and a B1 4-6-0 take their 1950s Halifax-Morecambe excursion over the viaduct at the north end of Crossley's mill before facing the steep climb up through Lee Bank Tunnel. This tunnel was so dark and smoky that the only way drivers could check they had not stalled was to reach out and touch the tunnel wall.

Crossley's Carpets at Dean Clough Mills had an extensive internal rail system which delivered coal to a large boiler house containing between eight and 10 boilers.

It also moved machinery between the mills and engineering workshops.

Wagons were horse-drawn but in later years a tractor with a large wooden draw beam was used.

Crossley's were said to be the world's top producer of broad loom carpets and their products were used in ocean liners and public buildings.

Closed after being ruthlessly taken over in the late 1960s, the mills are now split into business units but traces of the railway can still be found.

Top: Among the through freight trains which struggled over the "Alps" in LNER days was this heavy 7.10pm from Halifax, pictured being hauled through Ovenden station by ex-GN 0-6-0 No. 3006 and ex-Great Central Q4 0-8-0 No. 6175. *(Jack Wild collection)*

Centre: The timber station at Ovenden looking towards Holmfield in April, 1956, almost a year after closure but when the line was still used for freight and special traffic. The platform buildings lasted until 1963.

Bottom: The Queensbury line saw regular use by football specials. Here, B1 4-6-0 No. 61296 coasts down through Ovenden with a Bradford-Halifax special on 3rd March, 1951. *(Arthur Wilson)*

In 1953/4 three packed football specials left Halifax for a big match at Bradford Park Avenue. But 100 people were still left on the station so the station master called Sowerby Bridge shed to help make up another train. All they had was an ex-L&Y 2F 0-6-0ST.

The train set off at a snail's pace, stalled in Lee Bank Tunnel and near Holmfield was overtaken by a horse walking in a field. As it passed through Holmfield two men got off, went to the toilet and got back on again.

The Halifax supporters only just made it for half time.

Above: Holmfield station was on its last legs by the time this picture was taken in early 1955 of an N1 0-6-2T pausing there with a two-coach Halifax train. The bay once used by St. Paul's passenger trains is on the left while the slotted starting signal shows the all clear.

Below: The layout at Holmfield. *(Not to scale)*

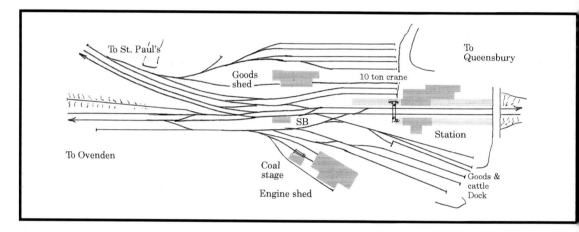

Below: Holmfield looking towards Halifax on a dismal day in early 1955, a day which sets the mood for impending closure. The goods yard on the right is still busy, though, and remained in business until June, 1960. The junction with the High Level Line going away to the right is situated between the goods shed and the 70-lever signal box.

In 1965 an Ovenden man wrote in the Halifax Courier of Holmfield: "I remember...green GN engines and the cry 'change for Pellon and St. Paul's."

"The goods yard was crammed with merchandise of all sorts. The cattle pens were used almost daily, cattle arriving on the front of passenger trains. "

In 1956 private sidings served Drakes Ltd.(off the St. Paul's line) and Shell-Mex & BP Ltd. (off the Ovenden line.)

Above: An L&Y 0-6-0 battles up the 1 in 53 from Holmfield and approaches Pellon with a local trip in 1959. Wheatley Viaduct is just visible beyond the engine. *(Arthur Wilson)*

Right Wheatley Goods, between Holmfield and Pellon, had a loop, one open siding, one to a small goods shed and one going into the Webster's brewery maltings, all to the left. But these wagons, looking towards Holmfield, were for lifting track after closure in 1960. *(John Rothera)*

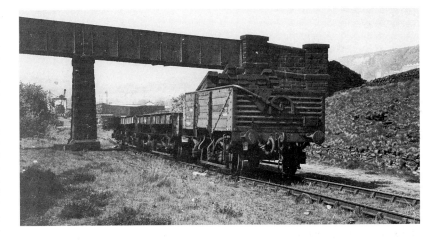

Below: Having just passed the disused station, WD No. 90412 enters the sprawling Pellon yard with a short goods in July, 1959. Behind it is Chambers' timber yard, still in business in 1998.

Above: Pellon yard in 1960, looking towards St. Paul's with the coal drops on the extreme left, the two-storey warehouse on the right, and the main line behind it. *(Jack Wild / S. Chapman collection)*

Pellon was a very cold place to work in but it was busy. Besides Chambers' timber yard siding, an incline went up to a Shell-BP oil depot. Most traffic was coal but there was a 10-ton yard crane, a cattle dock, a water tank for engines, and traffic included wool, steel, engineering products and machine tools. The passenger station entrance was on the bridge at the junction of Pellon Lane and Dyson Road. St. Paul's was dedicated to coal traffic once the passenger station had closed. Long after this Mackintosh's and Crossley's ran joint works outings to the seaside from St. Paul's and sometimes a circus train arrived there. Much of the High Level line is still traceable.

The last goods train ran to St. Paul's on 30th June, 1960. The Black Five 4-6-0 and its Sowerby Bridge crew, joined by the Halifax station master and the district inspector, went to collect empty wagons. It set off with just a brake van which it propelled from Holmfield to St. Paul's.

There, without ceremony and watched only by BR officials, a few children and a Halifax Courier reporter, it collected two wagons followed by another 24 from Pellon.

Chief clerk Arnold Collins told the Courier about Pellon's wartime heyday: 'Wheat was stockpiled at the start of the second world war, and railwaymen handled everything from foodstuffs to TNT during the war."

He talked of the 500 3cwt bales of wool still stored in the big warehouse, put there by government agencies during the Korean war. They would be moved to the London wool sales in November.

Below: Two hundred enthusiasts enjoyed a rareand final chance to visit Halifax St. Paul's by passenger train on 6th September, 1953 when N1 0-6-2T 69430 took the Stephenson and Manchester Locomotive societies' West Riding Railtour there. Because of the poor condition of the pointwork at St. Paul's, the engine ran round at Pellon and propelled the train to the terminus. *(M. Bland)*

Right: In 1958, 41 years after closure, the Halifax St. Paul's station concourse remained largely intact complete with ornate ironwork, if a bit scruffy with coal sacks draped over the barrier fence. Standard BR steel bodied 16-ton mineral wagons - nicknamed "tin cans"- fill the coal yard outside.

Below: The layout at St. Paul's. *(Not to scale)*

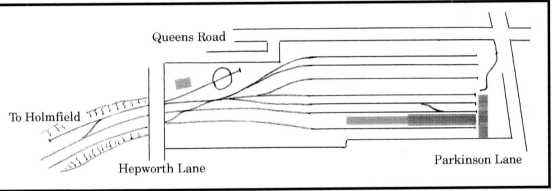

Right: The exterior of St. Paul's station buildings on 18th April, 1963, just after demolition work had started. *(Jack Wild / S. Chapman collection)*

In the days when the High Level line was fully signalled, it had a signal box at St. Paul's which was built into the rock cutting on the east side of the yard. Pellon had two boxes, one built into the rock cutting south west of the warehouse and one on the north side of the Pellon Lane overbridge.

In 1910 passenger trains left St. Paul's for Holmfield at 6.35am, 8.40, 10.12, 11.12MThO, 12.5pm SO, 1.12, 2.48, 3.5, 5.38, 6,17, 7.33 and 10.25. The journey took eight minutes to Holmfield and nine from Holmfield. Twelve trains also ran from Holmfield to St. Paul's. St. Paul's had seven staff then.

On its last day - Saturday 21st May, 1955 - the Queensbury line probably carried more passengers than since the day it opened as enthusiasts flocked to witness the last rites. One local remarked: "It's amazing how many folk turn out for a funeral." The last train from Halifax, at 7.30pm, was worked by N1 0-6-2T No. 69487.

By November, in a real-life Titfield Thunderbolt story, 180 villagers of isolated Harecroft mounted a drive to buy the line. Supported by other communities they set up the Bradford, Keighley and Halifax Rail Users' Committee. They won backing from 15 MPs including Clement Atlee and forced a debate in the House of Commons. But BR said the line was still needed for goods and special passenger trains. Villagers were angry because BR had not tried using more economical diesel Paytrains.

The sad end to a fascinating railway as dereliction sets in at Queensbury on 6th September, 1964. Above is a sign still advising passengers on the Keighley-Bradford side to change there for Halifax. The top picture shows railtour 1F52 forming the last passenger train of all to call there, on the same side(complete with cow) looking towards Bradford. After withdrawal of regular passenger services, Queensbury handled goods as a public delivery siding served from Bradford until that section closed altogether in November, 1963. *(Both Jack Wild / Stephen Chapman collection)*

Below: At 4.47pm on the last day of services, 21st May, 1955, N1 0-6-2T No. 69467 enters a somewhat rickety Queensbury station with the 4.18pm Keighley-Bradford. *(David Holmes)*

Above: The Red Bank vans 1980s-style. This was the Sunday Leeds to Red Bank working diverted from its normal route via Huddersfield and approaching Todmorden hauled by a single Class 31 diesel. Having just emerged from the 274-yard Horsfall Tunnel(partly rebuilt in early 1998), it is crossing Lob Mill Viaduct and is about to enter the 194-yard Castle Hill Tunnel. The spring points and runaway siding, designed to catch any wagons that might break away from a loose coupled freight train, were removed soon after this picture was taken. *(Oliver Chapman)*

MODERN MEMORIES

Trans-Pennine Expresses diverted via the Calder Valley, Sun. 17.11.85

11.19 09.51 York-Liverpool hauled by 45114
11.21 09.35 Liverpool-Glasgow hauled by
　　　　47408 *Finsbury Park*
11.30 11.12 Leeds-Red Bank vans Class 45
12.17 10.33 Liverpool-York hauled by 45108
13.15 11.51 York-Liverpool hauled by 45137
　　　　Bedfordshire & Hertfordshire Regiment TA
14.15 12.45 Liverpool-Newcastle　　45107
15.10 11.45 Newcastle-Liverpool　Class 45
16.15 14.48 Liverpool-Scarborough Class 47

Sunday 29th July, 1990 was typical of many when Trans-Pennine expresses were diverted over the Calder Valley. Class 47 No. 47434 *The Brontes of Haworth* approaches Milner Royd Junction signal box with the 09.00 Newcastle to Liverpool. Such diversions are still commonplace but no longer loco-hauled. *(Stephen Chapman)*

107

Top: On Sunday 17th April, 1988 the Trans-Pennine expresses were diverted via Bradford, Halifax and the Calder Valley because of engineering work at Heaton Lodge. Class 47 No. 47558 *Mayflower* accelerates the 08.00 Newcastle-Liverpool over Dryclough Junction. (*Stephen Chapman*)

Centre: For two seasons running Halifax reached the Rugby League Cup Final at Wembley, resulting in five special trains for supporters. Some empty stock came via Manchester and some via Healey Mills needing a pilot up the 1 in 45 bank from Greetland. On 2nd May, 1987 "Peak" No. 45066 was pilot, leading Class 47 No. 47452 towards the waiting fans. (*Stephen Chapman*)

Left: BR/Sulzer Type 2 diesels worked some Calder Valley freight until their demise in the late 1980s, even double-heading oil trains from Stanlow. No. 25257 passes Hebden Bridge with an eastbound train of Presflo cement wagons on 13th November, 1984. (*Alan Whitaker*)

Above: One of the most prolific trains on the Calder Valley in the 1980s and early 90s was the normally double-headed Lindsey Oil Refinery-Preston Docks petrol and bitumen train. The train ceased when the Petrofina petrol terminal at Preston closed. The bitumen tanks were attached to another train but only until the tar works at Preston also closed. Class 31s 31188 and 31317 pass the site of Brighouse Exchange sidings with the return empties in July, 1991. *(Stephen Chapman)*

Observations made at Todmorden on Tuesday 4th March, 1986 illustrate the level of daytime Calder Valley freight traffic at the time.
08.08: eastbound Class 47-hauled 100-tonne tanks; **10.39:** Stanlow to Jarrow tanks hauled by Class 56 56073; **11.58:** Newcastle to Red Bank vans hauled by 31272; **12.04:** Preston Docks to Lindsey tanks hauled by 31201 and 31407; **12.08:** Leeds to Stanlow empty tanks hauled by 25912 *Tamworth Castle* and 25903; **12.40:** empty Class 56-hauled coal wagons from Fiddlers Ferry; **12.50:** eastbound 100-tonne tanks hauled by 56058; **14.46:** empty coal wagons from Fiddlers Ferry hauled by 56129; **15.46** Class 47-hauled eastbound 100-tonne tanks; **16.11:** MGR coal to Fiddlers Ferry hauled by 56011.
Passenger services were a mixture of 2-car Class 110 'Calder Valley', 101, and 111 Metro-Cammell, and 108 'Derby' DMUs. Just one diagram used a 3-car 110. The 06.35 Hull-Manchester Victoria was a 2-car 600hp 101 running an hour late. The 09.32 from York was a Class 105 Cravens set.

Left: Mytholmroyd station looking east on 5th February, 1988 - around the time it was being described as West Yorkshire's worst public facility. Things were so bad that the elevated subway floor had collapsed and passengers had to cross by scaffolding and planks. A public meeting was held to decide what to do about it with the result that a new £400,000 station was built on the far end of the old one, just beyond the Class 142 Pacer forming a Manchester-York service. Being listed as a historical structure, the old buildings and canopy survive in 1998.
(Stephen Chapman)

Top: The eerie yet industrious scene inside Summit Tunnel in May, 1985 during repair work after the fire.
Repairs taking several months and costing £1.5 million included stabalising the lining with huge anchor bolts driven into the ground behind, strengthening support for two ventilation shafts and relining part of the tunnel with reinforced sprayed concrete as well as complete renewal of track, drainage and signalling. Three of the 14 ventilation shafts were filled with polyurethane foam and capped with concrete. The tunnel reopened on 19th August, 1985. *(Stephen Chapman)*

Left: No sooner had Summit Tunnel been put right than major problems hit Holme Tunnel at Copy Pit.
At 08.30 on 18th February, 1986 permanent way staff clearing icicles found serious structural defects in the 265-yard tunnel and the line was immediately closed, remaining shut until 13th October. The tunnel had been forced sideways by movement in the hill it passed through, distorting and cracking the lining. It had to be fitted with a steel rib cage to prevent further distortion, reducing clearances to the point where it was necessary to impose a severe speed restriction. Bars had to be fitted to the opening windows of the Class 104 DMUs operating the Leeds-Preston service so that no-one could stick their head out and hit it on the tunnel wall.
The distortion caused to the tunnel shows up well in this picture of the rib cage being installed. *(Stephen Chapman)*

Right: In March 1984 the heaviest freight train ever to cross the Pennines started running between the Shell refinery at Stanlow and its sister refinery on Teesside. Weighing 2,000 tonnes, the train of 18 bogie tankers carrying hot semi-refined oil, needed two Class 56 locomotives totalling 6,500hp. No 56106 was leading the pair over the Rochdale Canal bridge at Gauxholme on its way down from Summit Tunnel in June, 1984. Alas, while the tunnel was shut the Teesside refinery closed and the train stopped running. *(Stephen Chapman)*

Below: The last steam train on the Calder Valley Manchester line(so far) was this York to Heywood private charter crossing the canal bridge hauled by preserved Midland Compound 4-4-0 No. 1000 on 28th September, 1983. The Compounds once worked Blackpool trains via the Calder Valley. *(Fastline Photographic)*

Top: Long trains of 16-ton coal wagons are a once familiar sight which can no longer be seen anywhere on the main line network. This was actually a train of spent ballast from track renewal work at Walsden on 8th January, 1988. Being hauled towards Copy Pit by Class 47 No. 47340, the train has just emerged from the 290-yard Kitson Wood Tunnel.

Centre: In the late 1980s, BR occasionally replaced a failed DMU with a loco-hauled train. Here, Class 31 No. 31144 calls at Todmorden with the 18.23 Manchester Victoria-York on 20th August, 1990. The train left from Manchester Victoria's secret platform 17, unnumbered and hidden behind a wall.

Bottom: Despite 10 years talk of ten new stations in Calderdale only one has so far opened. The new Walsden is seen on opening day, 10th September, 1990. (*All Stephen Chapman*)